The Dark Side of Courtship

**SAGE SERIES ON
CLOSE RELATIONSHIPS**

Series Editors
Clyde Hendrick, Ph.D., and
Susan S. Hendrick, Ph.D.

In this series...

The Dark Side of Courtship

Physical and Sexual Aggression

Sally A. Lloyd
Beth C. Emery

Sage
Series
on Close
Relationships

Sage Publications, Inc.
International Educational and Professional Publisher
Thousand Oaks ■ London ■ New Delhi

For information:

Sage Publications, Inc.
2455 Teller Road
Thousand Oaks, California 91320
E-mail: order@sagepub.com

Sage Publications Ltd.
6 Bonhill Street
London EC2A 4PU
United Kingdom

Sage Publications India Pvt. Ltd.
M-32 Market
Greater Kailash I
New Delhi 110 048 India

Printed in the United States of America

Library of Congress Cataloging-in-Publication Data

Lloyd, Sally A.
   The dark side of courtship: Physical and sexual agression / by Sally A. Lloyd, Beth C. Emery.
   p. cm. — (Sage series on close relationships)
   Includes bibliographical references and index.
   ISBN 0-8039-7063-3 (cloth: acid-free paper)
   ISBN 0-8039-7064-1 (pbk: acid-free paper)
   1. Dating violence. 2. Courtship. I. Emery, Beth C. II. Title.
III. Series.
   HQ801.83 .L56 2000
   306.73—dc21

                                                    99-6749

00   01   02   03   04   05   06   7   6   5   4   3   2   1

Acquiring Editor:	Jim Brace-Thompson
Editorial Assistant:	Anna Howland
Production Editor:	Diana E. Axelsen
Editorial Assistant:	Victoria Cheng
Typesetter:	Christina M. Hill

Contents

Series Editors' Introduction

When we first began our work on love attitudes more than a decade ago, we did not know what to call our research area. In some ways, it represented an extension of earlier work in interpersonal attraction. Most of our scholarly models were psychologists (although sociologists had long been deeply involved in the areas of courtship and marriage), yet we sometimes felt as if our work had no professional "home." That has all changed. Our research not only has a home but also has an extended family, and the family is composed of relationships researchers. During the past decade, the discipline of close relationships (also called personal relationships and intimate relationships) has emerged, developed, and flourished.

Two aspects of close relationships research should be noted. The first is its rapid growth, resulting in numerous books, journals, handbooks, book series, and professional organizations. As fast as the field grows, the demand for even more research and knowledge seems to be ever increasing. Questions about close personal relationships still far exceed answers. The second noteworthy aspect of the new discipline of close relationships is its interdisciplinary nature. The field owes its vitality to scholars from communications, family studies and human development, psychology (clinical, counseling, developmental, social), and sociology, as well as other disciplines such as nursing and social work. It is this interdisciplinary wellspring that gives close relationships research its diversity and richness, qualities that we hope to achieve in the current series.

The **Sage Series on Close Relationships** is designed to acquaint diverse readers with the most up-to-date information about various topics in close relationships theory and research. Each volume in the series covers a particular topic or theme in one area of close relationships. Each book reviews the particular topic area, describes contemporary research in the area (including the authors' own work, where appropriate), and offers some suggestions for interesting research questions and/or real-world applications related to the topic. The volumes are designed to be appropriate for students and professionals in communication, family studies, psychology, sociology, and social work, among others. A basic assumption of the series is that the broad panorama of close relationships can best be portrayed by authors from multiple disciplines, so that the series cannot be "captured" by any single disciplinary bias.

Although our series has included books concerned with gender, conflict, and communication, the current volume very compellingly combines all three topics. In *The Dark Side of Courtship: Physical and Sexual Aggression,* Sally Lloyd and Beth Emery teach us more than we ever wanted to know about physical and sexual aggression in romantic relationships.

After outlining some of the relevant theory on relational aggression and building a framework influenced by feminist, relational, and social constructivist and discourse perspectives, the authors reveal the realities of physical and sexual aggression in relationships through women's own words. They place these words squarely within the framework of society's discourse about women, men, and relationships, reaffirming the power of words to shape our lives.

The authors exercise their empirical skills and yet somehow transcend them as they bring to the reader the real words and real stories of real women. The resulting narrative is a powerful and chilling read.

CLYDE HENDRICK
SUSAN S. HENDRICK
Series Editors

Acknowledgments

During our work on this project over a number of years, we have come to understand and value the true meaning of the words "collaboration" and "synergy." In academia today, the emphasis is on individually produced works and individual achievement. We continually ask "why?" because we both feel strongly that our best writing and thinking occurs when we work together. We are so fortunate to have discovered each other as synergistic research partners and close friends. Our styles are highly compatible. We often speak with a single voice yet maintain complementary areas of difference and strengths. By the time we finished researching and writing together for this project, we often could not tell who started and who finished an idea, thought, or sentence. It has been a delightful, exhilarating, and rewarding process.

We express our gratitude to many others who supported this work. Susan and Clyde Hendrick, the series editors, provided excellent feedback and critique of the manuscript and were incredibly encouraging over the extended time it took us to complete this volume. Terry Hendrix at Sage was equally patient and supportive. Miami University and the Human Sciences Department at Middle Tennessee State University were important players in the process as well, and we are grateful for the research leaves (we were able to arrange them simultaneously!) that provided the necessary time to complete this project. We also recognize the fine work and dedication of

Anne Castleton, Wendy Farmer, Michelle Herring, Robin Hughes, and Penny Reese, who assisted us in interviewing and transcribing. In addition, thanks go to Kim Kompel and Regina Adams, who spent many hours coding and providing valuable insights.

We do need to go back further in time in expressing our thanks. Early in our careers, we had the good fortune to work with Rodney Cate, June Henton, Scott Christopher, and Jim Koval. Our collaboration with them planted the seeds for our current emphasis on the interplay of romance, violence, and sexuality. Over the years, their continued support has been invaluable. Simultaneously, our involvement in the Feminism and Family Studies section of the National Council on Family Relations has provided us with a stimulating forum within which to integrate our disciplinary training with feminist frameworks. We are eternally grateful to our many feminist friends and colleagues who have enriched our work in untold ways.

We also must express our thanks to the three terrific people with whom we share our lives and homes, Charles Emery, Andrew Wong, and Alexander Lloyd Wong. We benefited greatly from their patience, understanding, and reading and discussion of our work. Their love and emotional support constituted a major commitment to this project!

Finally, our deepest gratitude goes to the 40 young women who shared their stories with us. Their courage has been our inspiration and the driving force behind this project. We are so very thankful for their willingness to be interviewed, for their passionate retelling of harrowing events, and for their deep desire to contribute to the prevention of physical and sexual violence against women. They asked us to tell their stories in the hope that other women would not have to experience the abuse that they did. We honor their request, in part, with this work. This book is dedicated to them.

1

❦

"I Never Thought It Would Happen to Me"

The Dark Side of Romance

Lisa[1] was 18, engaged, in the Marines, and, in her words, "young and stupid." While on a weekend trip with a group of fellow Marines and friends, she was raped by one of the men. He came to her room in the night, ignored her protests, and, holding her down, raped her. She slept on the couch the next night while another friend slept nearby to protect her. Her assailant was furious with her, dumping her clothes out into the snow. When she returned to base, she filed charges against him with the military authorities. Three days later, she was called in, read her rights, charged with slander and defamation of character, and told never to mention the incident again. She contracted physical complications from the rape, as well.

Her second aggressive experience occurred 5 years later. She had moved out of her boyfriend's house to regroup and think about their relationship. He was older and pushing for a commitment that made her uncomfortable. She had taken his laundry back to him and, during that visit, he asked her to marry him. Lisa asked for a couple of weeks to think about it and he snapped. "It was like his face iced over. . . . It was like looking at something out of a horror movie," she recalled. He then proceeded to tell her she would never leave alive and tried to kill her. Over the course of the next several hours, he attacked her with a knife, beat her severely, and raped her repeatedly. She eventually escaped to a neighbor's house and called the police. He was arrested, but when the case came to trial, the sexual assault and attempted murder charges were dropped. He spent 20 days in jail. She was subjected to harassment at her workplace and eventually moved away because of the whole episode.

Her third experience took place with her husband, who was abusive twice while they were dating (which caused a breakup for a while). After they married, he was jealous and very violent toward her. He would physically attack her and then force her to have sex. She divorced him after 8 months. Now she is extremely cautious in dating and very straightforward about her expectations and what she will and will not tolerate. Due to severe injuries sustained from the physical abuse, Lisa has a physical disability that makes it impossible for her to walk even short distances. She has been in counseling several times and, although she has many obstacles to overcome, she is moving forward in her life.

During the 1970s, largely due to the efforts of feminists, shelter workers, and victims of domestic violence, the issue of wife battering came to the forefront as a compelling social issue. It became increasingly clear that a problem that had once been thought to affect only a few women (and then only those women who did not count in our society—the poor and uneducated) actually affected a staggering number of wives—indeed, nearly one in four (Straus, Gelles, & Steinmetz, 1979). As the empirical studies stacked up, so too did the public outcry against the battering of wives by the very men who had promised to protect, honor, and love them.

Many of the early studies of wife abuse were studies of women who had sought shelter and protection from their husbands' violence. In several of these early shelter studies, the women noted that the battering had begun during their courtships (see, e.g., Dobash & Dobash, 1979; Walker, 1979), and, in fact, in some cases the abuse had been quite severe well before wedding vows were spoken. However, the problem of domestic violence was conceptualized early on as an issue that was present in marriage, or at the very least in long-term and semipermanent cohabiting relationships. In the first rush to understand the problem of physical and sexual aggression in intimate heterosexual relationships, the possibility that aggression began during dating and the early phases of the development of the relationship was largely ignored (there are some notable exceptions; see, e.g., Kanin, 1957; Pleck, 1987; Waller, 1937).

A study by James Makepeace (1981) served as an initial catalyst that forever changed the landscape of the domestic violence literature. Makepeace reported that 21% of college students had experienced or perpetrated an act of physical aggression in the context of a dating relationship. Makepeace's work was followed quickly by additional research on physical and sexual aggression that documented the startling incidence of aggression in both college- and high school-age dating relationships (Burcky, Reuterman, & Kopsky, 1988; Cate, Henton, Koval, Christopher, & Lloyd, 1982; Henton, Cate, Koval, Lloyd, & Christopher, 1983; Koss, Dinero, Seibel, & Cox, 1988; Koss & Oros, 1982; Laner & Thompson, 1982; Muehlenhard & Linton, 1987; O'Keefe, Brockopp, & Chew, 1986; Russell, 1984). After the initial identification of the social problem of physical and sexual aggression during courtship by these researchers, work on the topic exploded during the 1980s and 1990s. This research documented the incidence of aggression, as well as the personality, relationship, social structural, and attitudinal correlates of courtship aggression (e.g., Bergman, 1992; Browne, 1993; Canterbury, Grossman, & Lloyd, 1993; Christopher, Madura, & Weaver, 1998; Cook, 1995; Finley & Corty, 1993; Goodman, Koss, Fitzgerald, Russo, & Keita, 1993; Koss, 1993b; Small & Kerns, 1993; Stets & Pirog-Good, 1990).

As a result of the burgeoning interest in the topic, the body of research that has been conducted on physical and sexual aggression during courtship and dating is very large; rather than describe it all in detail, we offer a brief review of the major findings. This review covers the prevalence, correlates, and impact of aggression. We then outline how this book contributes to and extends current knowledge in the field.

❧ The Literature on Physical and Sexual Aggression in Courtship

The Prevalence of Courtship Aggression

Physical aggression typically is defined as "the use or threat of physical force or restraint carried out with the intent of causing pain or injury to another" (Sugarman & Hotaling, 1989, p. 4). Aggression is often operationalized, using the Conflict Tactics Scale (Straus, 1979), as the number of times the respondent had either enacted and/or received acts of pushing, shoving, slapping, kicking, biting, hitting with fists, hitting with an object, beatings, and threats/use of a weapon. Using such a definition, in a nationally representative sample of never-married individuals aged 18 to 30, Stets and Henderson (1991) found that 30% of the sample reported using and 31% reported receiving physical aggression during the past 12 months. An examination of aggression that occurs for teenagers revealed rates that are similarly high: Gray and Foshee (1997) examined the prevalence of physical aggression in the most recent or current dating relationship among students in Grades 6 through 12 and found rates of 36% using aggression and 34% receiving aggression. Looking at lifetime incidence and based on a wide variety of research studies, Sugarman and Hotaling (1989) calculated that 33% of men have been physically aggressive in a dating relationship and that 36% of women have been victims of physical aggression.

Statistics on the incidence and prevalence of sexual aggression paint an even more dismal picture. *Sexual aggression* typically is defined as sexual interaction that is gained against one's will through use of physical force, threat of force, pressure, use of alcohol/drugs, or use of position of authority (Koss, 1988). Between 6% and 28% of women report experiencing an acquaintance or date rape—intercourse that occurred in a situation of threat of or actual force (De-Keseredy & Schwartz, 1998; Kilpatrick, Best, Saunders, & Vernon, 1988; Korman & Leslie, 1982; Koss, 1993a; Koss, Gidycz, & Wisniewski, 1987; Muehlenhard & Linton, 1987; Russell, 1984). Expanding the definition of sexual aggression to include attempted rape or intercourse that occurred with coercion increases the proportion of women reporting sexual aggression to 39% (Koss, 1988). If all types of unwanted sexual interaction are included in the definition of sexual aggression (such as petting or kissing that is accompanied by coercion, pressure, or threats), 45% to 75% of women report being victimized (Browne, 1993; Burke, Stets, & Pirog-Good, 1989; DeKeseredy & Schwartz, 1998; Koss, 1988, 1993b; Small & Kerns, 1993).

The Correlates of Courtship Aggression

The correlates of courtship aggression can be classified into three categories: personality/individual, relational, and social/situational. In terms of personality and individual level factors, a fairly clear profile of the male abuser has arisen over the many studies of courtship aggression. The male physical abuser is likely to have low self-esteem, hold traditional attitudes toward women and male-female roles, be experiencing an increased level of stressful life events, have witnessed or experienced abuse in his family of origin (including heightened levels of corporal punishment), and hold both adversarial sexual beliefs and more accepting attitudes toward the use of violence (Barnes, Greenwood, & Sommer, 1991; Bookwala, Frieze, Smith, & Ryan, 1992; Burke et al., 1989; Deal & Wampler, 1986; Follingstad, Rutledge, Polek, & McNeil-Hawkins, 1988; Makepeace, 1987; Malone, Tyree, & O'Leary, 1989; O'Keefe, 1997, 1998; Simons, Lin, & Gordon, 1998; Smith & Williams, 1992; Worth, Matthews, & Coleman, 1990). The male sexual aggressor is likely to hold traditional beliefs about women and sexuality, display hostility toward women, believe that male-female relationships are adversarial, be "hypersexual" (i.e., report a high level of sexual partners and experiences), display intimacy deficits, show heightened levels of callous and exploitative psychopathy, be suspicious of his partner's communications, and believe in rape-supportive myths (Calhoun, Bernat, Clum, & Frame, 1997; Christopher et al., 1998; Christopher, Owens, & Strecker, 1993; Hersh & Gray-Little, 1998; Kanin, 1985; Kosson, Kelly, & White, 1997; Malamuth & Brown, 1994; Malamuth, Sockloskie, Koss, & Tanaka, 1991; Marshall & Hambley, 1996; Muehlenhard & Linton, 1988; Spitzberg, 1998; Stets & Pirog-Good, 1989). However, many of these characteristics of the aggressive male are considered "inconsistent risk markers," meaning that the evidence is somewhat mixed (Sugarman & Hotaling, 1989).

Female victims of physical and sexual aggression during courtship, on the other hand, do not display a personality profile, per se. Studies do not demonstrate consistent differences in assertiveness, feminist beliefs, or rape-supportive myths (Arias, Samios, & O'Leary, 1987; Korman & Leslie, 1982; Koss & Dinero, 1989; Lloyd, 1991). Most of the differences seen between women who have experienced aggression and those who have not experienced aggression are effects of the aggression itself (rather than risk factors). For example, the reactions to having experienced physical or sexual aggression include lowered self-esteem and sense of well-being; greater social isolation, stress, depression, and withdrawal; and symptoms associated with post-traumatic stress disorder (Browne, 1993; Coffey, Leitenberg, Henning, Bennett, & Jankowski, 1996; Shapiro & Schwarz, 1997; Zweig, Barber, & Eccles, 1997).

Relational factors are somewhat more consistent predictors of physical and sexual aggression (Lloyd & Emery, 1993). Ironically, the likelihood of male perpetration of physical and sexual aggression increases with the length and commitment of the relationship (Arias et al., 1987; Belknap, 1989; Burke et al., 1989; Hanley & O'Neill, 1997; Kanin, 1957; Stets and Pirog-Good, 1990). For the female partner, psychological commitment to the relationship can become a trap—the attraction to and investment in the relationship literally becomes too costly to forego (Rosen, 1996). Aggression often is precipitated by relational issues such as jealousy, relational insecurity, anger at the female partner, problem-solving dilemmas, perceived rejection, power struggles, and sexual denial (Bookwala & Zdaniuk, 1998; Foo & Margolin, 1995; Laner, 1983, 1990; Lloyd & Emery, 1994; Stets & Pirog-Good, 1989). In a conflict situation, male aggressors are characterized by negative affect, escalated conflict, miscommunication, attempts at domination and control, power struggles, restrictiveness/control, poor conflict skills, verbal aggression, emotional abuse, blaming the partner, eruptions of anger, a belief that the partner can be changed, and a belief that violence will result in winning the argument (Amick & Calhoun, 1987; Bird, Stith, & Schladale, 1991; Carey & Mongeau, 1996; Christopher et al., 1993, 1998; Emery & Lloyd, 1994; Foshee, Bauman, & Linder, 1999; Gryl, Stith, & Bird, 1991; Hamby, 1996; Lloyd, Koval, & Cate, 1989; Magdol, Moffitt, Caspi, & Silva, 1998; O'Keefe, 1997; Riggs & Caulfield, 1997; Riggs & O'Leary, 1996;

Ronfeldt, Kimerling, & Arias, 1998; Rosen & Bird, 1996; Stets & Pirog-Good, 1989).

Social/situational factors are also at play in the dynamics of courtship aggression. The social network appears to play a key role in sustaining and building norms for aggression. The male network, in particular, may reinforce the "appropriateness" of physical and sexual aggression against women (DeKeseredy, 1988, 1990; Drout, Becker, Bukkosy, & Mansell, 1994; Gwartney-Gibbs, Stockard, & Boehmer, 1987; Kanin, 1985; Schwartz & DeKeseredy, 1997; Stets, 1991). In some networks (e.g., those centered around fraternity membership or sports participation), the perpetration of sexual and physical aggression may be a male rite of passage of sorts, behavior that is not only encouraged but expected as proof of male prowess (Boswell & Spade, 1996; Copenhaver & Grauerholz, 1991; Martin & Hummer, 1998; Schaeffer & Nelson, 1993; Tyler, Hoyt, & Whitbeck, 1998; Worth et al., 1990).

Another key social/situational variable is the social isolation of both aggressor and victim. The aggression itself is likely to take place in private; even if the abuse does occur in a public place, others are unlikely to intervene (Cate & Lloyd, 1992; Laner, 1983; Roscoe & Benaske, 1985; Spitzberg, 1997). As a component of the abuse itself, the male aggressor may systematically cut his partner off from contact with family and friends, to prevent both discovery and help-seeking. The female victim also may try to hide her victimization from her network or downplay its severity out of embarrassment, a desire to preserve the network's good opinion of her partner, or fear of the consequences of disclosure (Emery & Lloyd, 1994).

Alcohol use is common to both physical and sexual aggression and is reported as a factor in 50% to 75% of the incidents of aggression (Abbey, Ross, McGuffie, & McAuslan, 1996; Canterbury et al., 1993; Hammock & Richardson, 1997; Leonard, 1999; Makepeace, 1981; Muehlenhard & Linton, 1987; Norris & Cubbins, 1992; Small & Kerns, 1993). Alcohol may serve as a disinhibitor of the aggressor's behavior, and/or as an excuse or reason for the aggressive behavior (Kantor & Straus, 1990).

Finally, there are some situational/contextual characteristics that affect sexual aggression in particular ways. These characteristics all revolve around the "script" for sexual interaction during dating. Male initiation of the date, male payment of the expenses, and the woman going to the male's apartment have been seen as signals of female compliance with male demands and as hints that the woman is desirous of sexual interaction. Indeed, both college-age and high school-age men believe that sexual aggression is more justified under such circumstances and sexual aggression is more likely to occur (Koss, 1988; Lundberg-Love & Geffner, 1989; Muehlenhard & Linton, 1987; Norris, Nurius, & Dimeff, 1996; Spitzberg, 1997, 1998).

The Impact of Courtship Aggression

What is the impact of physical and sexual violence that occurs during courtship and dating? Short-term effects include a range of emotional reactions, including fear, anger, withdrawal, and distress (Cate & Lloyd, 1992; Emery, Cate, Henton, & Andrews, 1987; Henton et al., 1983; Kilpatrick et al., 1988; Koss, 1993b); a variety of somatic complaints, including sleeplessness, headaches, gastrointestinal disorders, and pelvic pain (Kilpatrick et al., 1988; Koss, 1993b; Koss & Heslet, 1992); and physical injury, ranging from broken bones to concussion to vaginal tearing (Kurz, 1997; Stermac, DuMont, & Dunn, 1998). Long-term effects of sexual assault include depression, social phobia, sexual dysfunction, alcohol/drug abuse and dependence, and symptoms of posttraumatic stress disorder (Koss, 1993b; Koss, Heise, & Russo, 1997; Resick, 1993; Shapiro & Schwarz, 1997). Long-term effects of physical abuse include depression, heightened mistrust of men, wariness of signals of control, and redefinition of self and self-esteem (Lloyd & Emery, 1993). Finally, a particularly insidious long-term effect of courtship aggression is the heightened risk of subsequent victimization. For those couples who marry despite the presence of physical aggression during their courtships, the chances of continued physical aggression during their marriages are quite high (Bradbury & Lawrence, 1999; O'Leary et al., 1989). Finally, although the underlying mechanism for heightened risk is not fully understood, it is clear that women who are sexually victimized in adolescence or young adulthood are at greater risk of repeat sexual victimization later in their lives (Breitenbecher & Gidycz, 1998; Gidycz, Hanson, & Layman, 1995).

❧ Overview of This Volume

As can been seen in the brief review of the literature presented here, after nearly two decades of fairly intensive scrutiny, a great deal has been learned about physical and sexual aggression during courtship. What we have learned lends a particular urgency to our continued inquiry into this topic. We know that aggression is remarkably prevalent, affecting at least one third and perhaps more than one half of all dating partners. We know that physical and sexual aggression have very negative short- and long-term consequences for the victim. Furthermore, we know that for those relationships that progress to a legal commitment, the aggression that began during courtship is quite likely to continue into the marriage.

Yet, there are still important issues to be addressed in the study of courtship aggression. It is our hope that this book advances two critical arenas in the scholarship of courtship aggression: the integration of multiple theoretical perspectives to build a conceptual framework, and the importance of listening carefully to the voices and wisdom of women who have experienced aggression.

Chapter 2 presents our conceptual framework for the analysis and understanding of courtship aggression that builds on three perspectives: feminist, relational, and social constructivism. Although two of these perspectives (feminist and relational) have been applied in many studies to the analysis of aggression, the third (social constructivism) has not been used as often. Given that these perspectives often are viewed as antithetical to one another (particularly relational and feminist), our use of these three perspectives together is, we believe, somewhat unique.

Chapters 3 and 4 present the results of two qualitative studies of courtship aggression. Chapter 3 analyzes the narratives of 20 women who experienced physical aggression, and Chapter 4 analyzes the narratives of 23 women who experienced sexual aggression. In both chapters, we emphasize the relational dynamics that surrounded the perpetration of aggression, the issues of control, and how the women made sense and constructed meaning around these highly traumatic and unexpected occurrences in their courtship/dating relationships. In Chapter 5, we draw general conclusions about the roles of control and interpersonal communication and about the ways that women who have experienced aggression are powerfully silenced in multiple ways.

Thus, this book is intended to build on and extend our understanding of the dynamics of physical and sexual aggression in courtship by giving voice to the experiences of women who have experienced aggression. Their stories, insights, attempts to understand, and desire to warn other women about what can happen, even at the hands of one who purports to love you, form the foundation of this volume.

❧ Note

1. Throughout this volume, pseudonyms are utilized to protect anonymity.

2

❦

A Framework for Understanding Physical and Sexual Aggression in Courtship

Last week, I joined four female colleagues for our weekly lunch together. Our conversation, as always, focused as much on the personal as on work. That day, Jean was visibly upset. She told us about her 11-year-old niece, who had been attacked and sexually assaulted by a stranger. The niece and her family were on vacation, and the attack took place in a deserted hallway of the hotel where they were staying. The only thing that prevented the rape of the girl was the sudden appearance of her 9-year-old sister, who began screaming and scared the attacker off.

We tried to comfort and support Jean, who was worried sick about her nieces and her sister (their mom). We spent a lot of time talking about rape, sexual assault, fear, how these kids would cope with the experience of this attack, how lucky the niece was to have escaped being raped. And the whole time, I had this little sick feeling in my stomach—the same one I always get when women talk about rape—a little visceral reminder of my own experience of attempted rape.

And as is not uncommon in such discussions, we began to relay some of our personal experiences with sexual assault. I talked about waking up one night and realizing that a man was standing next to my bed. I too was lucky—my screaming scared him away (he did leave most of his clothing behind, though). Another woman described an attempted rape by a supervisor. A third told of her experience of date rape. And I thought, good heavens, four out of the five women at the table have had very frightening experiences with sexual assault. We all talked about fear—fear for ourselves, fear for friends, fear for daughters, fear of what women experience. Then we talked about anger—the anger that comes when you feel your life restricted and the anger that comes when at age 40 you sometimes are still afraid of the dark and have to sleep with the lights on when you are alone at night.

✌ Building a Framework

The influences on our own conceptual/theoretical approach to understanding aggression in courtship have been many and varied. First and foremost, part of our understanding is personal. This personal understanding is shaped every time a conversation like the one described in the beginning of this chapter occurs. It is expanded every time we interview a victim of sexual and physical aggression and hear her personal story. It is enlightened every time a student comes to us after class and says "Can I talk with you? I think I am being abused, and I don't know what to do." This book is premised on building a personal understanding by sharing women's experiences, in their own voices, throughout the volume.

Over time, we have found that three conceptual frameworks resonate with our experience: feminist, relational, and constructivist. Each of these frameworks provides unique meaning and understanding of the phenomenon of aggression during courtship. One irony is that these perspectives often are viewed as antithetical to one another. We make the case, as Bartle and Rosen (1994) and Goldner, Penn, Sheinberg, and Walker (1990) so eloquently do, that it is possible to retain feminist convictions and simultaneously examine the transactional patterns that sustain aggression in relationships. Goldner et al.

referred to this as a "both-and" framework, rejecting the notion that a forced choice between frameworks is required. Rather, they emphasized the freedom of movement that can be found between frameworks that are unfortunately often cast as immutable. We like to think in terms of taking what we find most useful from each framework and weaving them together so that the strength of one perspective is allowed to fill a gap that the limitations of another perspective may leave open. Just as there is no one truth, there is no one "best" perspective.

We describe our conceptual framework for understanding physical and sexual aggression in courtship to make explicit our "working assumptions." This builds on and expands the tenets we outlined for examining conflict and physical aggression in romantic relationships (see Lloyd & Emery, 1994) and is modeled after the working hypotheses presented by Goldner et al. (1990). We use scholarship on aggression against wives and on aggression against women in dating and courting relationships, for both of these literatures are helpful in building an understanding of the dynamics of physical and sexual aggression during courtship.

Before elaborating our conceptual framework, we first address how we conceptualize the issue of perpetrator and victim. We acknowledge that there is consistent evidence that both men and women engage in physically aggressive behavior during courtship (Stets & Henderson, 1991; Straus & Gelles, 1990). However, we believe it is overly simplistic to assert that men and women are "equally violent" without a close examination of the context and consequences that surround the use of aggression in intimate relationships (Bograd, 1990; Campbell, 1993; Currie, 1998; DeKeseredy, Saunders, Schwartz, & Alvi, 1997; Johnson, 1995; Ylló, 1988). First, women's use of violence occurs largely in self-defense—that is, in response to men's use of violence (Bograd, 1990; Jacobson et al., 1994; Saunders, 1988; Ylló, 1994). Second, women are clearly at much greater risk for injury, due to the greater size and strength of men, and men's use of more harm-inducing tactics of violence (Morse, 1995; Stets & Straus, 1990). Indeed, women sustain the vast majority (more than 95%) of the injuries that occur in situations of domestic violence (Langley, Martin, & Nada-Raja, 1997; Schwartz, 1987). Third, much of the prevailing scholarship on physical and sexual aggression in courtship does not

clearly address the issue of victim/perpetrator. Indeed, the methods
used to study these phenomena (e.g., the Conflict Tactics Scale [CTS];
Straus, 1979) emphasize the overall frequency of aggressive behaviors and do not clearly assess who initiated the aggression, who was
responding, who was responsible, or the longer-term context of the
relationship. Using data from such "blind" scales to state that women
and men are equally involved in the perpetration of aggression is
wildly inappropriate, given the limitations of the data (Currie, 1998;
Dobash, Dobash, Wilson, & Daly, 1992; Lloyd & Emery, 1994). Finally,
the overall context of romantic relationships is clearly one in which
men are empowered to hold dominance over women (DiLorio, 1989;
Dobash & Dobash, 1979; Dobash et al., 1992; Lloyd, 1991).

Based on these realities, we conceptualize aggression during courtship in terms of men's abuse of women. We do not deny that women
behave aggressively in romantic relationships, and we acknowledge
that there are situations in which the woman is the sole aggressor and
in which men do sustain injuries at the hands of their female partners
(Emery & Lloyd, 1994). Yet, the more likely dynamic is one of male
aggressor and female recipient (Bograd, 1990). As a result, in our
research for this volume, we frame courtship aggression in terms of
what we see as its most likely occurrence: male perpetrator and
female victim. As our explication of feminist and constructivist
frameworks bears out, our conceptualization of women as the likely
victims of aggression is integrally tied to our emphasis on the larger
context of aggression in romantic relationships—a context in which
notions of power, gender, control, and romance are critical.

≥⊛ Feminist Perspectives

It is difficult to describe "feminist theory" succinctly, because
the body of feminist thinking lies not in a singular theory but in a
series of perspectives or frameworks (Osmond & Thorne, 1993).
However, various feminist perspectives do share common themes:
assumption of the centrality and value of women's experiences,
examination of gender as socially constructed, analysis of gender
relations within specific historic and sociocultural contexts, rejection of a unitary notion of the family, and use of methodologies

that are value-committed and that emphasize social change (Osmond & Thorne, 1993).

Dobash and Dobash (1979) and Brownmiller (1975) contributed early on to a feminist analysis of wife abuse and rape, respectively. They challenged male domination within the family and described a system of patriarchy that legitimized aggression as a man's tactic of controlling a woman. They argued eloquently that the family, the criminal justice system, and the helping professions all serve as a systematic set of institutions embedded in a patriarchal system that serves to socially construct abuse as a woman's lot.

Bograd (1988) outlined four major dimensions of a feminist perspective on wife abuse. We find that her dimensions apply equally well to physical and sexual aggression in courtship. First, analyses of gender and power are critical components of a feminist perspective. Male-female relationships are structured by the unequal distribution of power, a distribution that affords men greater access to material and symbolic resources and devalues women and women's work and emphasizes women as sexual objects (Bograd, 1984; MacKinnon, 1982; Maynard, 1993; Muehlenhard, Danoff-Burg, & Powch, 1996). Patriarchy is a hierarchical system that maintains the "rights" of certain groups (white, heterosexual men) to define and control others (Baber & Allen, 1992; Knudson-Martin & Mahoney, 1996). Men may use aggression as a powerful means of subordinating women; indirectly, men as a class benefit from the ways in which the threat of aggression restricts women's lives and makes women dependent on men for protection (Beneke, 1982; Bograd, 1988; Breines & Gordon, 1983; Brownmiller, 1975; Harding, 1987; Koss & Cook, 1993; Muehlenhard et al., 1996).

Second, feminist frameworks emphasize that patriarchy influences even the most objective and abstract scholarship and theory development. This influence causes the experiences of women to be viewed as distorted or against the "norm" (the male perspective being normalized) or to be rendered invisible (Bograd, 1988; Griffin, 1981; Thompson, 1992). For example, Frazier and Seales (1997) argued that acquaintance rape is constructed as a woman giving in to a seduction that she later regrets by those who wish to diminish the overwhelming prevalence of women's experiences of sexual aggression. Yet, when the experiences of women become the centerpiece of scholarship and are told in their own frames of reference and with their own voices, a vastly different portrait of sexual assault emerges.

Third, Bograd (1988) pointed out that feminist scholarship is scholarship for women rather than about them. For example, feminists are particularly concerned about challenging the ways that women are blamed for the aggression that is directed toward them (Emery & Lloyd, 1994; Kelly, 1988a; Maynard, 1993). Sandra Harding (1987) discussed the implications of research that takes the perspective of women as primarily that of victims. Although it serves to refocus the responsibility for the aggression on men (something that is also done elegantly by Mike Johnson's [1995], term "patriarchal terrorism"), such research creates limitations by perpetuating a false impression that women are only reactive in their abusive situations. Feminist scholars consistently document that women do resist domination and abuse (Emery & Lloyd, 1994; Kelly, 1988a; Lempert, 1996; Mahoney, 1994). Ultimately, use of a feminist framework not only reflects women's experiences but also advocates for social and theoretical change (Breines & Gordon, 1983; Browne, 1993; Kirkwood, 1993; Maynard, 1993; Stanko, 1997; Thompson, 1992; Thompson & Walker, 1995; Yllö, 1994).

Fourth, feminists question the notion of the family as a haven in a heartless world (Bograd, 1988). Rather, the family (and, we would add, heterosexual, romantic relationships) are viewed as part and parcel of the power structure that has contributed to women's subordination and oppression (Kirkwood, 1993; Knudson-Martin & Mahoney, 1998). Although women ostensibly appear to hold a dominant position in the family and in relationships, the reality is that they may have control only over the things that are of little consequence to their partners—that is, those things traditionally defined as "domestic" (Baber & Allen, 1992). A historical legacy of legal "ownership" of women by their husbands, fathers, and boyfriends, coupled with a long tradition of differential access to resources, the isolation of the intimate dyad, and specialized male and female roles, have helped lay the foundation for a relational ideology that emphasizes the legitimacy of male dominance over women (Bograd, 1988; Coontz, 1992; Kelly, 1988b; Kirkwood, 1993; Pleck, 1987). This male dominance is manifested both as hostile sexism—for example, angry and derogatory comments about women—and as passive sexism—protective paternalism (Glick & Fiske, 1997).

Nowhere is this dominance more visible than in men's use of physical and sexual aggression as a tactic of coercive control of women (Dobash & Dobash, 1979; Lloyd & Emery, 1994; Serra, 1993). Indeed, "the primary intent and function of battering is the intimidation and control of another" (Gortner, Gollan, & Jacobson, 1997, p. 347). This control may entail literal physical control of her person—for example, holding her down, locking her in a room, or forcing intercourse— as well as psychological or symbolic control—fear, degradation, or denial of her independence of thought and behavior (Campbell, 1993; Goldner et al., 1990; Griffin, 1981; Kirkwood, 1993; Marshall, 1994; Stets & Pirog-Good, 1990; Umberson, Anderson, Glick, & Shapiro, 1998; Wiehe & Richards, 1995). Physical and sexual aggression may be used as tactics to get what he wants, to strike fear into the victim, to intimidate her, to retaliate against her autonomous actions, and to maintain "order" (Emery & Lloyd, 1994). Male aggressors provide a variety of control-related "explanations" for their aggression, including the need to dominate the woman, fear of her gaining independence, fear of abandonment, her failure to live up to the obligations of being a "good woman," jealousy over interaction with other men or family members, spending decisions, and sexual denial (Blixeth, 1987; Dutton, 1988; Dutton & Golant, 1995; Lloyd & Emery, 1994; Maynard, 1993; Ptacek, 1988; Stets, 1988). Over time, control tactics may form a vicious web, as the control of the abuser is strengthened by the victim's lowered self-esteem, loss of separate identity, hopelessness, and depression (Avni, 1991b; Kirkwood, 1993; Wiehe & Richards, 1995).

Our emphasis on aggression as an act of control is not meant to ignore the simultaneously highly expressive nature of an act of violence. Indeed, aggressive men often speak of losing control, of not even remembering what occurred in a "blind rage," of "drowning in a red tide" of anger, or of being caught in a wave of sexual passion (Beneke, 1982; Dutton & Golant, 1995; Goldner et al., 1990; Stets, 1988). Aggression often occurs in a context of volatile, negative interaction and is accompanied by belligerence and extreme anger, all of which clearly speak to its expressive side (Lloyd, in press). We disagree with the notion, however, that violence is instrumental or expressive. Rather, like Goldner et al. (1990), we argue that aggression can be simultaneously an expressive and an instrumental action; even when aggression is experienced by the man as a frightening loss of emotional control or as an uncontrollable sexual impulse, his aggression has an instrumental control-based underlying intent. Indeed, Dutton and Golant (1995) noted that battering is not a random act, as a purely expressive model might suggest; it is an act of rage directed at a very specific person (the female partner) and at a very specific time (e.g., after a perceived transgression such as talking to another man), and only in specific locations (at home, or when no observers are present). Koss and Cleveland (1997) similarly noted that date rape is fraught with intentionality; sexually aggressive men use alcohol and seduction tactics to reduce resistance and choose "fair targets" (e.g. , a woman dressed "provocatively"). In doing so, the men's culpability is reduced.

Thus, physical and sexual aggression are problems that have developed out of a social structure of patriarchy, which enforces traditional gender relations both in marriage and in courtship (Maynard, 1993). Powerful gender injunctions set the stage for our intimate relationships and "virtually prescribe male domination and female subjugation" (Goldner et al., 1990, p. 350). Ultimately, aggression is both "an expression and a mechanism of the institutional oppression of women" (Kirkwood, 1993, p. 21).

A feminist orientation pervades our work in multiple ways. Our feminist lens leads us to examine issues of male control and women's oppression, sociocultural and historical contexts, and the ways that patriarchal ideologies contribute to the construction of traditional gender relations in courtship. We agree with Rosen and Bird's (1996) statement that "the patriarchal structure of our society is an aspect of the political that cannot be ignored when examining and intervening in men's violence against women" (p. 319). Our feminist perspective formed the basis for the methodology we chose and the questions we asked, and it shaped our interpretation of the stories we heard from the women we interviewed. As feminists, we place a high priority on women's experiences and women's voices.

❧ Relational Perspectives

The second body of work that has influenced our conceptualizations of physical and sexual aggression in courtship is loosely termed "relational perspectives." This set of perspectives examines the interpersonal dynamics that both surround the use of aggression and characterize the overall relationship between perpetrator and victim (Cahn, 1996; Giles-Sims, 1983; Lloyd, in press; Spitzberg, 1997). Relational perspectives also emphasize the phenomenology of actors, including the accounts they give to explain why aggression occurs, their explanations to excuse and justify the use of violence, and the ways that blame and responsibility are assigned (Felson & Tedeschi, 1993). Ultimately, a relational perspective allows us to acknowledge that "although contextual processes shape violence against women, the violence is inflicted and experienced in the lives of individuals" (Rosen & Bird, 1996, p. 319).

Our relational perspective draws from both systems theory and communication research on the dynamics of aggression. Systems perspectives seek to highlight interrelationships and transactions (Whitchurch & Constantine, 1993). Here, aggression can be viewed as a transactional pattern; for example, aggression can be seen as the product of a sequence of interactions characterized by negative reciprocity, volatility, rigid communication patterns, and/or attempts at domination (Burman, John, & Margolin, 1992; Lloyd, 1996; Margolin, John, & Gleberman, 1988; Rogers, Castleton, & Lloyd, 1996; Sabourin, 1995). Ultimately, aggression is simultaneously a coercive clash and an interpersonal message (Serra, 1993).

A cautionary note is required, however, because systems frameworks have been applied in such a way as to render the aggressive behavior, and the gendered nature of aggression, invisible (Bograd, 1984; Pare, 1996; Yllö, 1994). For example, systems perspectives may lead to a trap of thinking that all components contribute equally to the aggressive behavior—which confounds placing responsibility with the perpetrator of aggression (Dell, 1989; Kaufman, 1992; Kurz, 1998; Whitchurch & Constantine, 1993; Willbach, 1989). Yet, according to some feminist scholars (Bartle & Rosen, 1994, Bograd, 1984, Goldner et al., 1990), it is possible to integrate a "feminist-systems-relational" perspective by acknowledging the gendered nature of aggression, keeping male responsibility at the forefront, and acknowledging the patriarchal context of relationships that serves as an overlay for aggression.

Giles-Sims (1983) constructed one of the first explicitly systems-oriented models of wife battering that remained sensitive to this context. She highlighted the reinforcement patterns that help set aggression into a transactional pattern. Aggression "works" because it achieves a goal; when the perpetrator gets what he wants, he is quite likely to use aggression again in similar situations (Campbell, 1993; Giles-Sims, 1983). The eruption of aggression is also reinforced by the release of tension and the decrease in the "bad feelings" that led up to the battering (Dutton & Golant, 1995). The victim of aggression has few options in responding to aggression. If she uses self-defensive tactics, his aggression may escalate; if she responds with compliance or withdrawal, she may inadvertently reinforce his use of aggression through the process of negative reinforcement (Giles-Sims, 1983; Lloyd & Emery, 1994).

Systems perspectives also can be used to explicate the multiple mechanisms that are put into place to enact male control over the relationship. The world of the abused woman may be a family system wherein self-determination is not tolerated, relational rules are unilaterally established, and boundaries are tightly controlled by the abuser (Avni, 1991b; Bartle & Rosen, 1994; Bograd, 1984). The woman comes to define herself as the man sees her—dependent, doubtful of her abilities and sanity, worthless, and needing his protection (Avni, 1991b; Kirkwood, 1993). Such systems of "patriarchal terrorism" highlight the systemic and intentional nature of the abuser's actions to control his wife (Johnson, 1995).

The work described previously, which uses a contextualized systems perspective on male use of aggression against the women they love, is complemented by recent investigations of premarital communication patterns. Courting relationships with physically aggressive men are characterized by heightened levels of escalated conflict, verbal aggression, emotional abuse, anger tactics, attempts at domination and control, dissatisfaction with relationship power, and a belief that aggression will help win arguments (Bird et al., 1991; Carey & Mongeau, 1996; Hamby, 1996; Magdol et al., 1998; Riggs & Caulfield,

1997; Ronfeldt et al., 1998). Relationship experiences are also important in predicting the likelihood of male sexual aggressiveness: Such aggressiveness is predicted directly by relational conflict, miscommunication about sexual intent, ambivalence, and a desire for interpersonal control, and indirectly by anger and lack of empathy (Christopher et al., 1993, 1998; Motley & Reeder, 1995; Muehlenhard & Hollabaugh, 1988; Stets & Pirog-Good, 1989).

Our relational perspective also draws on research on marital interaction that emphasizes fine-grained analysis of communication patterns. This work clearly documents that patterns of dominance and negativity are key variables in understanding the dynamics of aggression. For example, physically aggressive husbands enact higher levels of threat, blame, and other offensive negative behaviors (e.g., signs of dismissal, pointing one's finger, waving arms, or negative physical contact) than do nonaggressive husbands. Aggressive husbands are high in overt hostility, defensiveness, and anger-reactivity, and low in problem-solving skills (Anglin & Holtzworth-Munroe, 1997; Burman, Margolin, & John, 1993; Infante, Chandler, & Rudd, 1989; Margolin, Burman, & John, 1989). They use highly provocative forms of anger, including belligerence and contempt; they are also unlikely to acknowledge that there is anything wrong with their behavior. Their wives, in contrast, although showing intense anger, also display high levels of fear, tension, and sadness (Jacobson et al., 1994).

Coan, Gottman, Babcock, and Jacobson (1997) examined dominance patterns in two types of battering men. Type I batterers exhibit a "bat-'em-back tendency"; even low level negative affect from the wife (e.g., complaint, sadness, anger) is batted back, with an "in-your-face" quality of high-intensity negative affect. Type I husbands rarely say anything conciliatory; instead, they enact patterns of belligerent control aimed at restraining the wife's requests for cooperation and expression of anger, and maximizing her feelings of fear (Gottman et al., 1995).

Coan et al. (1997) speculated that these Type I batterers are locked into an "honor code" that equates accepting influence from the wife with being unmasculine. They may feel compelled to reject all attempts at influence on the part of their wives, not only because of a pathological desire to control their wives but also as part of the belief that it is their right to do so (Coan et al., 1997). On the other hand,

Type II batterers reject only the highly negative communications from their wives; they appear to be threatened by the independence of their wives and fearful of abandonment and may have become abusive in an attempt to keep them from pulling away emotionally (Coan et al., 1997). Their wives responded with both acceptance and rejection of the negative affect, reflecting a pattern of both fear and resistance to his domination.

The tie between socialization for masculinity and battering also has been noted by Goldner et al. (1990) and Levant (1995a). They asserted that men who are aggressive toward women hold rigid premises about gender, including a belief that they must be stronger than women, that they must not be afraid or sad, that all things feminine should be avoided, and that intimacy is dangerous. Ultimately, aggression may be the means for a man to establish himself as a strong, masculine, and powerful person, a means of maintaining a particular system of gender patterns. As Goldner et al. noted, "Relationships in which women are abused are not unique but, rather, exemplify in extremis the stereotypical gender arrangements that structure intimacy between men and women" (p. 344).

In summary, a relational orientation pervades our work in multiple ways. It can be seen particularly in the analysis of the qualitative interviews, as we examine the dynamics that surround the man's use of aggression and the woman's response to his aggression. Overall, we advocate a contextualized, feminist approach to a relational framework that emphasizes the importance of not losing sight of the gendered nature of the perpetration of physical and sexual aggression nor of the larger patriarchal systems that support the use of aggression against women. In such a context, relational thinking can help to explicate the patterns of interaction that reinforce the use of physical and sexual aggression in courtship and dating.

❧ Social Constructivist and Discourse Contributions

A third major influence on our conceptualization of physical and sexual aggression during courtship is the work of social constructivists, who emphasize the role of discourse. We identify this as an area of analysis that is sorely lacking in the literature on the dark side of courtship. We hope to highlight the ways that our social constructions of both intimate relationships and aggression influence not only how victims and perpetrators construct meaning around aggression in their close relationships but also how significant others (i.e., family and friends) react to the occurrence of aggression.

Social constructivist frameworks are concerned with the ways in which meaning is socially constructed from everyday interaction, conversation, and assumptions (Berger & Kellner, 1970; Gubrium & Holstein, 1993a, 1993b; Holstein & Gubrium, 1995; Knudson-Martin & Mahoney, 1996; Pare, 1996; Reiss, 1981; Weingarten, 1991). Constructivism holds that knowledge is constructed within the context of its development or environment, and as we change meaning and behavior, we also change events. This change creates new issues, new problems, and an ongoing, cyclical process (Fisher, 1991).

Our social constructions of events are reflected in our discourse about those events. Hare-Mustin (1994) defined *discourse* as "a system of statements, practices, and institutional structures that share common values . . . the medium that provides the words and ideas for thought and speech, as well as the cultural practices involving related concepts and behaviors" (p. 19). Discourses serve to create meaning across time and context and to build a particular worldview (Hare-Mustin, 1994; Weingarten, 1991). Knudson-Martin and Mahoney (1996) used the language of "collective stories" to describe marital discourses in terms of societal values, norms, and ways of thinking about how to behave in relationships. Often, our marital discourse relies on a rather traditional and idealized view of heterosexual relationships—the family as natural and universal, functional and moral: the marriage as it "should be" (Gubrium & Holstein, 1990; Hare-Mustin, 1994).

Marital and family discourses are not constructed in isolation and are not immutable; they are inherently socially constructed over time through our interaction with others and are patterned along factors such as race, class, and gender (Yllö, 1994) and power (Hollway, 1989). Feminist approaches to the study of relationships and families are highly compatible with constructivism, for "the aim of the feminist critique is to point to a different way of constructing reality . . . [and that] existing reality is socially constructed along gender lines and must be reconstructed to give expression to women's experiences" (Delanty, 1997, pp. 117-118).

We believe that many parallels can be drawn from the literature on family and marital discourse to develop a more thorough understanding of the discourse of courtship and the discourse of aggression. Such an analysis is critical to advancing our understanding of physical and sexual aggression. As Ylö (1994) noted, the relationships between men and women in families carry worldviews that are particularly prone to sexist stereotypes. The examination of the predominant discourses on courtship and aggression can provide a context for understanding the prevailing mores and values that surround romantic relationships and the powerful role of invisible relational ideologies that influence the ways in which meaning is constructed around incidents of physical and sexual aggression (Hare-Mustin, 1994). As we seek to create understanding and meaning from such unthinkable and unanticipated experiences, our language serves to reflect the dominant discourses that are a nonconscious part of our identities as relational partners (Hare-Mustin, 1994; Knudson-Martin & Mahoney, 1998). As we seek surcease from family and friends, here, too, the discourses of relationships can serve to constrain the meanings that are constructed toward those who perpetuate the dominant ideologies about men and women, sexuality, romance, and courtship.

The Discourse of Courtship

There are three arenas of discourse that we feel are most endemic to constructing meaning and making sense out of courtship experiences. These are power and the myth of equality between the genders; romance; and sexuality.

Power and the Myth of Equality Between the Genders.   Power is a primary focus of feminist inquiry as well as a pivotal component to understanding relationship discourses. We draw heavily from Weedon's (1987) work on feminism and poststructuralism in our discussion of power. Discourses are relational, but not necessarily in the simplistic sense of powerful and powerless. They are described by Foucault

(1978) as elements that operate within relations of class, race, gender, religion, and age, for example, all of which have roots in social institutions. What becomes important to the examination of aggression in courtship is the additional fact that not all discourses derive their power from traditional social institutions. For example, feminist discourse conflicts with that of patriarchy yet creates the opportunity for resistance to the dominant subject positions and their social construction and regulation. In other words, as Foucault noted,

> Discourse transmits and produces power; it reinforces it but it also undermines and exposes it, renders it fragile and makes it possible to thwart it. In like manner, silence and secrecy are a shelter for power, anchoring its prohibitions, but they also loosen its hold and provide for relatively obscure areas of tolerance. (p. 101)

Weedon (1987) wrote that resistance by individuals to dominant discourses is the initial step in forming alternatives to that knowledge and/or believing in those marginalized discourses, which increases their social power. This has particular application to our work, in that we are interested in how women who have experienced aggression construct meaning around the event. In examining their discussions, we hope to determine which discursive interactions come to bear in their interpretations and rationalizations of the aggression. As power relates to the women in our studies, "it is exercised within discourses in the ways in which they [the discourses] constitute and govern individual subjects" (Weedon, 1987, p. 113). Interestingly, it is the mechanisms of power at the individual level that then become part of the dominant networks of power relations (Sawicki, 1991).

Foucault (1978), in discussing the repressive and productive natures of power, said, "Power is tolerable only on condition that it mask a substantial part of itself. Its success is proportional to its ability to hide its own mechanisms" (p. 86). Applied to relationships, one of the primary ways that power disguises itself in courtship and marriage is through the "myth of equality between the sexes" (Hare-Mustin, 1994; Knudson-Martin & Mahoney, 1998). The widespread discourse on "marriage between equals" serves as a cover for the presence of male domination in intimate relationships (Hare-Mustin,

1994) and allows couples to create an illusion of equality that masks the inequities in their relationship (Knudson-Martin & Mahoney, 1996). The discourse of equality operates in multiple ways. On the one hand, this discourse stresses natural differences between men and women; by viewing differences as ingrained, inequalities are no longer problematic, because each partner is doing that for which he or she is "best suited" (Hare-Mustin, 1994). On the other hand, the myth of equality may be constructed in a relationship as a way to avoid confronting the dilemmas of gender socialization and institutional inequities (Knudson-Martin & Mahoney, 1998). Indeed, because much of gender socialization operates below full consciousness, couples are often unaware of how it affects their behavior—from patterns of conflict negotiation to different premises for entering relationships (Knudson-Martin & Mahoney, 1996).

Certainly, this discourse affects relationships between men and women long before the wedding vows are uttered; we argue that courtship is viewed even more so as a relationship between equals to make palatable the patriarchal context. Courtship is characterized by a cultural milieu that emphasizes that women are the lovers and men are the leavers (Peplau, 1994; Rubin, Peplau, & Hill, 1981); the overriding importance of relationships to the personal fulfillment of women (Breines & Gordon, 1983; Knudson-Martin & Mahoney, 1996; Tannen, 1990); and a balance of power that still favors men (Avni, 1991a; DiLorio, 1989; Schwartz & DeKeseredy, 1997; Sprecher & Felmlee, 1997). These meanings contribute to a discourse that emphasizes male control of the activities and course of courtship in trade for the greater female need for a protective and committed relationship, as the "natural complementarity" that contributes to a balanced and equitable relationship between the genders.

The discourse of equality between the genders provides a particular context for the attribution of meaning to the occurrence of physical and sexual aggression. The emphasis on male control may be used to justify his use of force, for he may be interpreted as seeking only his natural right to be in charge of the relationship. And the emphasis on female dependence on a relationship may lead to an attribution that "even a violent man is better than none," which may constrain her to remain in the relationship lest she fall victim to the perils of an unattached state (Lloyd, 1991).

Romance. The discourse of romance is a second compelling feature of our language about courtship. The language of romanticism includes the notions of love at first sight, love as blind, love as magical, love as able to solve all relationship problems (as long as there is enough of it), and the idea that the stresses of courtship will go away as soon as marriage takes place (Notz, 1984; Pare, 1996; Waller, 1951). In a context of romanticism, partners are encouraged to attribute negative interaction to external forces—to overlook, forgive, or ignore negativity and conflict as atypical (Henton et al., 1983; Lloyd, 1991). "You and me against the world" may have particular meaning for the couple as a metaphor for what is right within the relationship and what is wrong with everything else.

Karen Rosen (1996), who studied the ties that bind women in abusive premarital relationships, might call this romanticism part of the process of seduction. Young women are drawn into relationships by romantic fantasies that result in their dependence and tolerance of negative behavior such as abuse. Romantic fantasies are similar to popular fairy tales such as *Cinderella* and *Beauty and the Beast*. In these fictional tales, Cinderella's drab life and insecurities are addressed and transformed by Prince Charming. The focus of the Beauty and the Beast fantasy is the vulnerability of the Beast, whereas it is the woman who transforms his life and, hence, her own (Rosen, 1996). These fantasies are played out all too often in dating relationships in which women are seduced into remaining with their Prince Charming at great physical and emotional risk. In the case of Beauty and the Beast, the woman stays because she wants to be that one person who can change him through her understanding and love. If she tries hard enough, love will conquer all.

Again, we are confronted with another popular discourse that puts forth the idea that women are responsible for the relationship (Campbell, 1993). These discursive aspects of gendered perspectives on relationships emphasize that maintenance chores are attributed to women and autonomous motives to men. In other words, men and women are empowered differently by romance and, therefore, are given contrasting positions and identities (Wetherell, 1995). This difference further serves to reinforce these romantic fantasies. It also serves to keep women in dangerous relationships when they should get out (Emery & Lloyd, 1994).

Romance also can be seen similarly in the popular literature as a text that presents an image of redemption, salvation, and rescue (Wetherell, 1995). In popular culture's film and fiction, it is the end of the story. It ties up all the loose relationship strings of ambiguity with a predictable ending that "stifles other interpretations and imposes its authority over other accounts" (Wetherell, 1995, pp. 132-133). One such example is the movie *Pretty Woman*, in which, in the end, the happy couple rides off in a limousine. Romance novels consistently end at the point where "boy gets girl" and they are assumed to live happily ever after. This is a static image that causes one to wonder about the stress created by the juxtaposition of the realities of life and images of romance. Much literature points to the contribution of relationship, emotional, academic, and financial stress to the use of violence in dating relationships (Emery, 1987; Makepeace, 1983; Mason & Blankenship, 1987). When some people begin to view their relationships in terms of "it's not supposed to be like this," does a punch come next? In other words, what contribution to the use of violence does the inevitable loss of the "rose-colored glasses" have?

Another issue that may come to bear on the discourse of romance is the fear of love's end. To fall out of love or romance is not just the loss of a relationship but the loss of a language, a discursive method of defining oneself and the other person and putting the two together (Wetherell, 1995). We take on a romantic "paradigm" of emotion, a model and a rationale for feeling and action. Although romance is supposed to be highly individual, it is also part of the culture, and, by taking on this paradigm, individuals affirm their place in society as well as support their culture. When we fall out of love or the relationship ends, the feelings of distress may have root in the loss of the paradigm or concept of love and romance as much as in the loss of a person or relationship.

Ultimately, the discourse of romance provides a way to make sense out of the paradox of physical and sexual aggression that occurs within the context of an intimate and caring relationship. Because romantic ideals embrace a "love conquers all" ideology, there is a strong push to forgive and forget (remember the classic line from the movie *Love Story*—"Love means never having to say you're sorry"?). Yet, forgiving and forgetting a transgression as major as aggression may not be so easy; indeed, the only recourse is to remove the blame from the perpetrator by attaching interpretations such as "He did not mean to do it" or "He's under so much stress that he just lost control." Indeed, both victims and perpetrators of courtship aggression are much more likely to attach an external meaning to the aggressive behavior than they are to view the behavior as an individual's responsibility. Is it any wonder, then, that aggression and love coexist in relationships (Cate et al., 1982; Goldner et al., 1990; Henton et al., 1983; Rosen & Bird, 1996)?

Sexuality. Sexuality is a third arena of the discourse on courtship that has important implications for making sense of aggression. Hare-Mustin (1994) described the male sexual drive discourse as so familiar as to be accorded the status of common sense. This discourse (which is also identified as the traditional sexual script) reflects the expectation that men have an urgent sex drive that must be fulfilled, that men should be the initiators of sexual interaction, that men may "lose control" when it comes to meeting their sexual needs, that men may be aggressive in seeking to satisfy sexual urges, and that women are expected to fulfill men's sexual needs (Byers, 1996; Check & Malamuth, 1983; Griffin, 1981; Kalor, 1993; Levant, 1995b; Metts & Spitzberg, 1996; Motley & Reeder, 1995; Muehlenhard & Hollabaugh, 1988). Men are expected to be dominant, and women are accorded the role of passive subordinate, provocative tease, or naysayer. In any event, her role is that of regulating his moral conduct (Burkhart & Stanton, 1988; Hare-Mustin, 1994). Clearly, these views of sexuality arise from and reinforce patriarchal structures in courtship.

The discourse of sexuality also includes the view that women's resistance to sexual pressure is token—women say "No" but they really mean "Yes" (Muehlenhard & Hollabaugh, 1988). Our notions about permissiveness serve to complicate the discourse of sexuality; although permissiveness ostensibly gives both men and women permission to engage in sexual expression, for men, it allows freedom of access, whereas for women, it may mean pressure to acquiesce to men's requests for sexual interaction (Hare-Mustin, 1994). Hare-Mustin asserted that the permissiveness discourse provides "no space for unwanted sex" (p. 27), because an urging toward compliance with male initiatives is also a part of permissiveness.

The discourse of sexuality is very potent, as individuals attribute meaning to and make sense of sexual aggression. Like the discourse of romance, the discourse of sexuality can easily be used to excuse his behavior ("He could not control his urges") and blame the victim ("She led him on," or "She should have known that's how men are"). Furthermore, given the pervasiveness of permissiveness language, it may be difficult to believe that in this sexually open age, she did not actually consent to the sexual interaction.

The discourses of romance and sexuality form an interesting juxtaposition. Wetherell (1995) declared that the discourse of romance is gendered. It is a story that women are supposed to want and men to reject; men are supposed to do sex and women do romance. Certainly, this discourse holds true when looking at classic sexuality research, which states that women view sex in terms of love (i.e., romance) and men in terms of recreation (Ehrmann, 1959; Peplau, Rubin, & Hill, 1977). The implications are clear for dating relationships. When mixed messages regarding sex occur, coercion may be the result. Although women may not be sure that the situation and circumstances are right (i.e., the relationship has not progressed to an appropriate level of commitment), men are trying to initiate sex. This describes, again in part, the traditional sexual script (Byers, 1996).

Although romance may seem to erase power in its image of mutuality and equality, the reality remains that in sexual interaction, men are often the initiators and women the receivers. This image of passivity on the part of women serves to create confusion and contradiction regarding sex within both individuals and the relationship. Any teenager can recite the rhetoric of the day regarding this dance of courtship intimacy. If she does not say "No," then she means "Yes," and if she does say "No," she still means "Yes," because "nice girls" are supposed to say no and to wait until they are in a loving, committed relationship before they have sex. Then, of course, according to the discourse of courtship, it is up to the man to initiate sex, and so the cycle continues. In fact, in recent years, our students have described to us a phenomenon called "relationship fraud." Young men have calculatingly created elaborate dating scenarios that are tailored to appeal to their female targets' ideals of romance. Once the woman has had sex with the man, he abandons the pretense of the relationship and the woman.

The Discourse of Aggression

Although physical and sexual aggression in romantic relationships has been a social problem of fairly recent interest, conversations on aggression and explanations for its occurrence are readily available. We identify four arenas of discourse that are commonly used in making sense of men's physical and sexual aggression against women. These are excusing the aggressor, blaming the victim, the debate over the definition of aggression, and rendering intimate aggression invisible.

Excusing the Aggressor. Our discourse on the causes of aggression often serves to excuse the aggressor for his actions. As noted in our discussion of the discourse of sexuality, due to the pervasiveness of the traditional sexual script, it is very easy to attribute date rape and sexual coercion to "sexual misunderstandings" or scenarios wherein the woman really desired sex but did not feel she could be so bold as to come right out and say so. Physical aggression can be similarly excused as a "loss of control." Indeed, when describing the reasons for their aggression, male perpetrators often talk about the feeling of being "out of control." These men describe their behavior as impulsive and full of emotion, even to the point of not being able to predict what will happen next or to remember the sequence of events that resulted in their physically or sexually assaulting the woman (Dutton & Golant, 1995; Stets, 1988). Such explanations also are reflected in popular notions about why domestic violence occurs; often, the behavior is attributed to a lack of psychological or sexual control. Ironically, if he has lost control, we are simultaneously off the hook in holding him accountable and able to blame his victim for making him lose control. Rarely in the popular discourse of aggression is there conversation about aggression as an instrumental action by a man to force a woman's compliance with his wishes.

Blaming aggression on a lack of control is but one of the many ways that our discourse about intimate aggression holds the perpetrator harmless for his aggression against a woman. Another equally popular explanation is the intergenerational transmission of violence; in this metaphor, his use of aggression is a reflection of the aggression he was exposed to or experienced as a child (O'Leary, 1988; Simons et al., 1998; Spitzberg, 1997). He is held harmless because he was never exposed to appropriate models or techniques for handling relationship conflict and maintaining a close relationship with a woman; in other words, he simply did not know better. The cycle of violence explanation abounds as we explain involvement in everything from violent criminal activity to perpetration of sexual abuse to incarceration (Widom, 1989). Indeed, the cycle of violence explanation has passed from a tendency noted in the literature to a social certainty; no small wonder that the popular literature rarely notes that the intergenerational transmission rate is only in the range of 20% to 30% (Kaufman & Zigler, 1987; Widom, 1989).

Blaming the Victim. An integral component of excusing the aggressor is the discourse of blaming the victim. From the classic question asked of the rape victim ("What were you wearing?") to the idea that physical aggression is merely a transactional pattern that arises from the behavior of both husband and wife ("What did you do to make him so mad?"), myriad ways abound to make the responsibility for aggression at least partially hers. Furthermore, as the women in our studies so clearly demonstrated, these efforts to encourage victim-blaming seem to work very well, for the vast majority of our interviewees engaged in self-recrimination and self-blame for being in the wrong place, for going out with the wrong type of man, for making the man angry, and ultimately for the aggression that he directed at her.

Because the dominant discourse specifies that the victim is responsible for the aggressive behavior, the result for victims is tantamount to revictimization. This time, the victimization is in the form of psychological abuse at the hands of the institutions of our society. As many women discuss their experiences with law enforcement officials, social workers, family, and friends, they report feeling a sense of betrayal. When they are pressed for proof of their assault, disbelieved, and shunned, they have in fact been betrayed and marginalized, as discourse theorists would say, by the dominant discourse within our society that asks what she did to deserve this behavior or tells her that this is all just part of how romantic relationships are.

The legal system depends on physical proof to define violence, and social scientists depend on objectivity and statistics to lend credibility to findings. (There are exceptions to this trend, specifically, feminist researchers and advocates who vehemently protest this androcentric, positivist approach.) To see the issue more clearly and to keep from "revictimizing" these women, we must ask ourselves "Who makes up the rules?"

Clearly, there is a long history of blaming the victims of both domestic violence and sexual assault, beginning with early depictions of female victims as masochistic and extending to more recent views of aggression that render power and gender invisible (Bograd, 1988). Although very blatant victim-blaming has abated, subtle forms still exist. One of the more subtle forms is linguistic avoidance; Lamb (1991) and Lamb and Keon (1995) noted that in both professional journals and newspapers, the majority of the references to "domestic aggression" are made in terms that leave the issue of male perpetration and female victimization fuzzy at best. In this way, assigning responsibility to men for their perpetration of violence against women can be avoided. References to violence against women in the media are largely made in the passive voice, a phenomenon that is associated with men attributing less harm to the victim and less responsibility to the perpetrator (Henley, Miller, & Beazley, 1995). In addition, the news media tend to dichotomize women who have been beaten, raped, or murdered by intimate partners into good girls versus bad girls, with the result that unless she was totally helpless (i.e., too old or too young to fight back), she is represented as somehow responsible for the attack (Meyers, 1997).

An interesting study by Foshee and Linder (1997) further demonstrates that attributions of blame are important variables to consider in the study of violence. These authors examined the factors that influenced service providers' motivations to help victims of violence. They discovered that service providers were much less likely to be willing to help female victims when the women were seen as provoking the violence by using insults. This unwillingness to serve was not seen for male victims who were perceived as provoking the violence, a finding that Foshee and Linder interpreted as reflecting that providers consider that female victims "get what they deserve."

The Debate Over the Definition of Aggression. Another way that emphasis is taken away from the victims and survivors of aggression is through the controversy over how to "define" aggression in the first place (Currie, 1998). Mary Maynard (1993) identified three kinds of definitions. The legal definition is behaviorally based; it is the narrowest, because it determines when the criminal justice and social welfare systems may intervene. The professional/expert definition is based on evidence collected regardless of the views of the victims, because many times women deny their experiences (e.g., out of fear of retaliation or naïveté). Finally, the definition by women who have experienced violence provides the broadest continuum, including acts ranging from threatening looks to seriously injurious behavior. This last category, the definition of the women themselves, is least used and valued. From Maynard's types, it becomes clear that a definition is, in part, a function of its application. If this is the case, it is important to ask whose constructions of violence and aggression "count," and why. Ultimately, shouldn't the discussion of violence extend beyond the debate over the "expert" definition of violence to include women's interpretations of their experiences as part of that definition?

One theme that emerges from both legal and expert definitions is a reluctance to label a particular behavior as rape or violence when it occurs within the context of a close relationship. For example, there is an entire body of literature that debates the existence of "acquaintance" rape (see chapters by Gilbert, 1993, and Koss & Cook, 1993, which present opposing views). Even the term *date rape* has been at issue, sometimes considered an oxymoron because of relationship context. This perspective sees dating as a relationship of reciprocity and pleasure, whereas rape is about violence and powerlessness. Date rape, or "rapette," thus is portrayed as not as traumatic as an act perpetrated by a stranger (Estrich, 1987; Koss & Cook, 1993). Victims may be equally reluctant or unable to define behaviors as rape or violence when they occur in intimate relationships (Emery & Lloyd, 1994; Kelly, 1988a). It would seem, then, that we may not even recognize the extent to which sexual coercion is a part of courtship because it is construed as a "usual" aspect of intimate relationships.

We believe that the dominant discourse of aggression denies women the ability to voice their experiences. They are thereby marginalized by the lack of an appropriate or existent vocabulary. The very words, labels, and expressions for their experience do not exist

(Bernard, 1987; Kelly, 1988a). The opportunity to identify what has happened is limited by the context of the dominant discourse of the time. It is one that is pervasively patriarchal, based on what "he" knows and what "he" is, in other words, a male worldview. Women's experience and discourse of violence are ones of subordination.

In response, we believe that to obtain an accurate understanding of violence in intimate relationships, and to break out of the constructions of aggression that render gender and power dynamics invisible, it is important not to place limitations on women's narratives. Preconceived and commonplace definitions of violence do this by reflecting men's ideas of what is acceptable or unacceptable and what is extreme behavior on the part of men (Maynard, 1993). Liz Kelly (1988b) stated in her book *Surviving Sexual Violence,*

> It is in men's interests, as the perpetrators of sexual violence, that definitions of forms of sexual violence be as limited as possible. At the same time as women are unable to name their abuse as abuse, men are able to deny responsibility for abusive behaviour. Language is a further means of controlling women. (p. 156)

Rendering Intimate Aggression Invisible. Finally, the extent of domestic aggression, and the vulnerability of all women to being exploited sexually and/or physically, are silenced in popular discourse by an emphasis on aggression as a problem that is rare and likely to occur at the hands of a stranger. Aggression is all too often portrayed as a problem that affects marginalized groups (e.g., poor women and women of color) and women of "questionable character" (i.e., women who somehow deserved to be beaten or raped). The overwhelming emphasis is on aggression as something that is unlikely to be experienced at the hands of a trusted intimate partner (Estrich, 1987). Physical and sexual aggression are simply not things that happen to "nice women"—and they are not perpetrated by men who purport to love them (witness the public disbelief of the evidence that O. J. Simpson had battered his wife, Nicole Brown Simpson). When nice men abuse nice women, the public outcry reflects concern about the violation of our collective story about intimate aggression as much as it reflects concern for the woman who has been victimized.

That the men who aggress against women strive to render women's victimization invisible is chillingly apparent in a study done by Lora Lempert (1996). She noted that the abuser uses a variety of strategies to hide his aggression. He may assert his privilege of ownership in regard to "his woman," he may control assaults by ensuring that abuse takes place in private and injuries are not obvious, he may isolate the woman and restrict her communication with others, and he may deny his responsibility and reconstruct the abuse as her fault (Lempert, 1996).

This loops our discussion back to the discourse of power. Recall that according to Foucault (1978), power is most successful when it can be rendered invisible. The implications for the discourse of relationship aggression are vast, for it leads to the understanding that not only must the victim of aggression be silenced, but the power of the male perpetrator must be well disguised. Social institutions such as the legal system, family, government, medicine, and the welfare system all collude in this silencing, for these institutions exist within a patriarchal structure that has constructed abuse as a "woman's lot" and therefore as a normal part of a romantic relationship.

Ultimately, this leads us to examine the social construction of courtship and aggression based on gendered positions because "the production of knowledge is not neutral, but is the consequence, as well as the condition, of power relations" (Hollway, 1989, p. 30). Research indicates that women do perceive themselves to be more vulnerable to violence (particularly rape) than do men (Gordon & Riger, 1989; Koss & Cook, 1993; O'Leary & Curley, 1986). Women change their lifestyles to protect themselves. They do not walk alone at night, they avoid certain areas of campus or town, and they install additional locks on the doors of their homes (Estrich, 1987).

What emerges from these two different responses to violence are seemingly complementary roles. The man (in accordance with the masculine subject position of the dominant discourse) is confident of personal safety and the ability to protect himself and women from physical harm, a role that coexists comfortably with the female position (consistent with her subjectivity of femininity within the dominant discourse) of vulnerability and dependence on the man for protection. As part of the discourse of aggression, these perceptions are reinforced by our culture.

It is ironic, then, that the real threat of harm to women is not the strangers from whom they so arduously try to protect themselves, but those who are already in their lives and homes and who are closest to them (Hickman & Muehlenhard, 1997; Kelly, 1988a; Koss & Cook, 1993). The focus on "stranger" attacks serves to successfully divert attention from the boyfriend, lover, or husband. Perhaps it is too painful and difficult to recognize that the real source of threat can be from loved ones. Or perhaps the overwhelming focus on stranger violence is merely a way to render invisible the true power of men in intimate relationships to harm the women they love.

Overall, then, the discourse of courtship and the discourse of aggression provide a context in which aggressors, victims, friends and family, and helping professionals construct meaning around physical and sexual aggression in courtship. We believe that the discourse of courtship encourages interpretations of physical and sexual aggression that are couched in the language of the myth of equality, the male sexual drive, and the romantic ideal. Furthermore, the discourse of aggression is likely to excuse the man for his aggression, blame the woman for provoking him, silence her definition of violence, and render intimate aggression invisible.

A constructivist orientation is threaded through our work in several ways. Essentially, our choice to interview women who have been victims of physical and sexual violence provides the foundation for a narrative analysis of their stories. The discourse of courtship and aggression provides a backdrop for our analysis of the women's narratives; in essence, it provides a context within which we place their stories. Our analysis emphasizes both how the women construct meaning around their experiences as well as the ways in which the discourse of courtship and the discourse of aggression are reflected in their narratives.

❧ Summary and Conceptual Model

In this chapter, we elaborated the feminist, relational, and constructivist perspectives that form our framework for looking at sexual and physical aggression during courtship. This elaboration is important in a narrative study such as ours, for it identifies the working assumptions upon which we rely as we seek to understand and construct meaning around the women's stories of the abuse they experienced, how they resisted it, and how they coped with the aftermath (see Figure 2.1 for a pictorial representation of our working assumptions and frameworks).

Common threads run through our discussion of the perspectives. One of the primary themes is the importance of examining power and control issues. How are power and control constructed in these relationships? When asked what the abuser was trying to accomplish, do the women speak in the language of control? What tactics do the women use to resist control? Ultimately, we are interested in the communication and construction of power, how it is accomplished and maintained, and how those who have experienced the misuse of power make sense of it and talk about it.

We are also highly interested in how the occurrence of aggression fits into the fabric of the relationship between the man and the woman; in other words, how does the political context of patriarchy become personal and individual within a given relationship (Rosen & Bird, 1996)? How do women who have suffered aggression describe other facets of their relationships with their abusers? What are their interpersonal dynamics? Do issues of dominance arise as the women describe their relationships with their abusers? How do these women frame the precipitators of his abusive behavior? How do they frame the impact of the abuse on the quality of their relationships?

Finally, we are interested in the ways in which the discourse of courtship and the discourse of domestic violence are reflected in the narratives that the women provide of their experiences of abuse. Do women who have been victimized use metaphors of romance? Do the women ascribe blame to themselves, and strive to forgive the abuser? Do they speak in terms that signal the invisibility of abuse ("I never thought it would happen to me!")? How do friends and family influence the constructions that the women make about their abusive relationships? Ultimately, what helps the women make "sense" of the abuse, understand it, and heal from it?

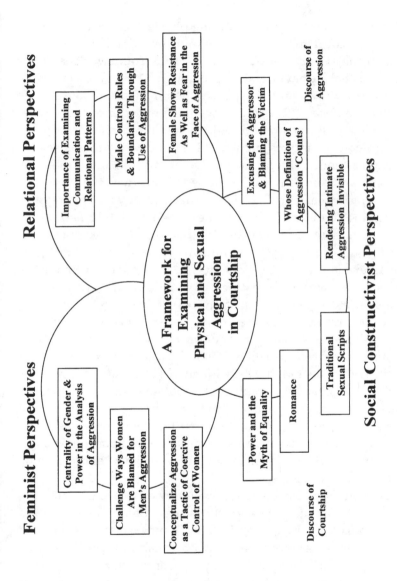

Figure 2.1. Theoretical Frameworks

Feminist Perspectives

- Centrality of Gender & Power in the Analysis of Aggression
- Challenge Ways Women Are Blamed for Men's Aggression
- Conceptualize Aggression as a Tactic of Coercive Control of Women

Relational Perspectives

- Importance of Examining Communication and Relational Patterns
- Male Controls Rules & Boundaries Through Use of Aggression
- Female Shows Resistance As Well as Fear in the Face of Aggression

Social Constructivist Perspectives

- Excusing the Aggressor & Blaming the Victim
- Whose Definition of Aggression 'Counts'
- Rendering Intimate Aggression Invisible
- Traditional Sexual Scripts
- Romance
- Power and the Myth of Equality

Discourse of Aggression

Discourse of Courtship

A Framework for Examining Physical and Sexual Aggression in Courtship

❧ Choosing a Method and an Analysis Strategy for the Study of the Dark Side of Courtship

The method we chose for studying physical and sexual aggression during courtship and the way that we frame both questions and analysis are natural outgrowths of the frameworks and assumptions that we have detailed previously. Our method is clearly feminist and draws on the aspects of feminist methodology outlined by Thompson (1992): It uses women's experiences as a source of knowledge, it attempts to make a connected relationship between researcher and researched, it is politicized in the sense that the feminist underpinnings are clearly laid forth, and it relies on discourse and subjectivity. We hoped to uncover the meaning-making that female survivors of sexual and physical aggression engaged in as they struggled to make sense of their traumatic experiences at the hands of a loved one. The analysis we engaged in contains not only components of feminism in its emphasis on issues of power and control but also elements of a relational view that is interested in uncovering the patterns, dynamics, and ways that male aggression and female victimization are sustained in relationships.

This book draws on an analysis of in-depth interviews with 40 women who were physically and/or sexually victimized by a man in a dating or courtship situation. Following the lead of Dobash and Dobash (1979), Bograd (1988), Kirkwood (1993), and many other feminist researchers, we conducted qualitative studies to help us explicate the complex dynamics that accompany physical and sexual aggression and to bring to the forefront the voices of women who have survived such experiences. Thus, the reflections, knowledge, and meaning-making of women who have survived abuse provide the key data for this book.

In both studies, all the women we interviewed were volunteers. Recruitment took place through flyers posted around campus and through calls for participation in family studies courses. The flyer calling for participation in the study of physical aggression started with the question "Have you (or are you) in an abusive relationship?" and went on to explain that we were interested in talking with women who had experienced physical violence in a dating or courtship relationship. The flyer recruiting women for the study of sexual aggression was similar but emphasized that we wished to talk with women who had experienced sexual aggression in a dating or courting situation. All of the women were attending one of two universities at the time of the interviews (a medium-sized southeastern university and a large urban university in the West). The women ranged in age from 18 to 38 and were predominantly European American, middle-class, and single. Thirty-nine of the 40 women interviewed had ended their relationships with the abuser by the time of our interviews. Their relationships had ranged from 9 months to 4 years in duration.

Interviews lasted between 1 and 3 hours, with an average length of 110 minutes. The interview questions were semistructured to allow the women to tell their stories in their own words and in their own way (interview questions for both studies appear in Appendix A and Appendix B). All of the physical aggression interviews were conducted first ($n = 17$).[1] As a way to assist in their recall of what had happened, the women completed a modified version of the CTS (Straus, 1979). The interviewer explored with the women their recounting of the first and the most recent abusive incidents, the types and extent of the abusive behavior, the dynamics that contributed to it, and what the abusive behavior meant to both the victim and the perpetrator. We then turned to the sexual aggression interviews. This time as an aid in recall we used the Sexual Experiences Survey (Koss, 1988). The interviewer asked the women to tell their stories, including the first and most recent times that sexual aggression had occurred, what they thought the aggressor hoped to accomplish, whether physical aggression was experienced as well, and the effect of sexual aggression on them and on their subsequent relationships. All interviews were audiotaped, and subsequently transcribed, with all identifying names, dates, and places deleted.

Data analysis used the qualitative methods outlined by Allen (1989), Glaser and Strauss (1967), and Strauss and Corbin (1990). Throughout, the emphasis was on understanding the data in context. Thus, rather than a microanalysis of simple utterances or sentences, what we sought was a careful reading of the interviews and the consideration of any given piece of text within the overall context of the entire interview (see Gavey, 1992). Our emphasis was on discerning the meaning and impact of the experience of physical and sexual violence for these women.

We used an iterative, open-coding procedure (as contrasted with a more quantitatively based content analysis). First, each of the three coders (the two authors of this volume and one graduate student) read the transcripts a number of times to become familiar with them. These initial readings were followed by extensive conversation as to the very broad themes that each of us saw in the transcripts. We then separately reread the transcripts, this time noting where common themes emerged across the women's stories. Essentially, each of us at that point wrote "field notes" on the transcripts, noting the categories we saw emerging. We then engaged in conversations once again, which served as a cross-comparison of similarities and differences in what we saw in the transcripts, and questioned one another's assumptions and analysis. This questioning covered not only the specific portions of the text we were coding but also whether the interpretations were consistent with the overall context of a particular interview. We continued by making associative connections across categories and collapsing fine-grained categories into broader themes. This iterative process of reading, note-taking, and comparative conversation continued until we felt that a common set of themes emerged from our joint construction of the transcripts and our ongoing conversation. Our team approach resulted in extensive discussion, some debate, and eventually a shared conceptual analysis (for more extensive discussion of this analysis strategy and its advantages, see Glaser & Strauss, 1967; Strauss & Corbin, 1990).

The remainder of this book presents our findings from the two sets of interviews. Chapter 3 addresses the dynamics of physical aggression during courtship, Chapter 4 addresses the dynamics of sexual aggression during courtship, and Chapter 5 presents conclusions and implications for intervention.

Our analysis in each chapter does not begin with a review of the literature, nor does it attempt to test any literature-based hypotheses. Rather, after letting the primary themes emerge from the analysis, we discuss the ways in which these women's narratives support existing literature on aggression, as well as the ways that their meaning-making dovetails with the predominant discourse on physical and sexual aggression during courtship.

Before recounting their stories, we express our heartfelt gratitude to the women who volunteered to be interviewed. This book is dedicated to them. We learned so much from them and with them, and we hope we can convey the deep respect we have for their courage, insight, bravery, and willingness to share their stories of harrowing experiences, as well as their strength and survival in the face of betrayal.

❧ Note

1. The number of interviews analyzed for physical aggression (the results presented in Chapter 3) was 20, because 3 of the women interviewed for the sexual aggression study also provided information on a relationship that contained primarily physical aggression.

3

❦

"I Wouldn't Hurt You If I Didn't Love You So Much"
The Dynamics of Physical Aggression

Maryanne was 16, a sophomore in high school, when she started dating Gary, who was older (20), good-looking, and popular. In the early part of their relationship, there was no physical violence; yet, Gary was very overbearing and commanding—a "Yes, you will" type of guy.

Gary and Maryanne started living together when she was 17. The first time that Gary was violent toward Maryanne was after he saw her talking to two guys while she was waiting for him to pick her up from high school. When she got into the car, he did not say a word. She had no idea it was coming. When they got back to their apartment, he caught her on the jaw and hit her up against the wall. Maryanne couldn't cry or scream or anything. Gary picked her up and threw her against the wall and then started yelling and screaming that he didn't want her talking with other guys. Then he threw her on the floor and locked her in the room.

Gary was extremely jealous and would get violent whenever he believed another guy was interested in Maryanne. He beat her when other men paid attention to her (he waited until they got home to start the beating, though). He accused her of having an affair with her boss. He broke her teeth, fractured four of her ribs, gave her numerous black eyes, fractured her nose, and caused hearing and kidney damage with his punches.

Maryanne did not know where to turn for help. She and her parents had fallen out over the relationship with Gary, and she now was living with him in another state where she knew no one. After the school incident, he forced her to drop out of school, and while she was working he constantly checked up on her. She was scared to death.

One night after Gary beat her up, she barricaded herself in the bedroom. She knew that he and a friend were going out drinking, and she waited until they came back and passed out before she snuck out. She went to a telephone booth and called her mom and asked her to come get her. She sat in the phone booth all night, and her mother drove the 400 miles in 6 hours, picked her up, and took her back to the safety of their family home. Her parents helped her file a restraining order and supported her as she went back to high school.

After telling her story, Maryanne poignantly commented, "I never saw myself as a teenager after that. You know, I had been through way too much that my classmates would ever think about going through."

After listening to the voices of 20 women who relayed this and similar stories of physical and psychological harm, we remain in awe of the strength and survivorship of each and every one of the women we interviewed. What they conveyed to us were their deeply personal feelings of betrayal by someone they loved, of confusion over how to make sense out of this unexpected occurrence, and of the myriad ways that the experience of abuse affected their lives and relationships.

This chapter emphasizes what we learned from the women about their experiences of physical aggression during courtship. The chapter is broken into four primary components: (a) a description of the physical aggression experienced; (b) the relational dynamics of physical abuse, including catalysts, communication dynamics, responding to the man's aggression, and the aftermath of aggression; (c) the dynamics of control; and (d) the ways in which the women talked about, defined, and constructed meaning around the abuse they had experienced, with a particular emphasis on how they came to blame themselves for the occurrence of abuse. The interconnectedness of our analysis of the relational dynamics, the dynamics of control, and the ways of constructing meaning is depicted in Figure 3.1. This figure

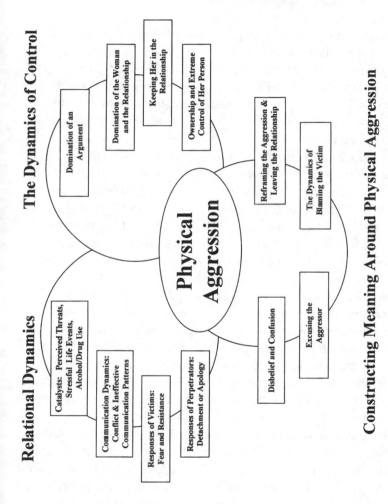

Figure 3.1. Physical Aggression

47

also reflects the three major components of the conceptual framework that we outlined in the previous chapter.

The Physical Aggression Experiences

Before we present our analysis of the 20 women's narratives, it is important to place those narratives in context by providing some background on the women in our sample. The women were white and predominately middle-class; 17 were enrolled in college at the time of the interview. Their average age at the time of the interview was 21 (ranging from 19 to 28 years). All had been involved in an abusive, heterosexual dating relationship with an average length of just over 2 years (ranging from 9 months to 4 years). Given the age of the interviewees and the length of their relationships, it is important to note that the abuse they experienced began at an average age of 17 to 18 years (ranging from 15 to 26 years old). Two of the women had been married to the abuser; 18 of the women were involved in what they termed as serious, committed dating relationships. At the time of the interview, 19 of the women were no longer involved with the man who had abused them.

There was a wide range of abusive behaviors reported by the women (see Table 3.1 for the mean number of behaviors reported). The most common act of aggression by the men was throwing, kicking, or smashing something ($M = 28.5$ incidents), followed by pushing, grabbing, and shoving ($M = 24.5$), and slapping on the body ($M = 11.3$). The most common act of aggression by the women was slapping on the body ($M = 10.3$), followed by pushing, grabbing, and shoving ($M = 9.7$).

The figures on mean numbers of acts are misleading if viewed only in the aggregate for men and women. What is more telling is an analysis of the men's and the women's use of aggression in tandem. Table 3.2 indicates that 10 of the women reported that their partners had been the only aggressive person in the relationship, and 10 reported "mutual" violence. The types of abusive behavior were broken down using a modified version of Straus's (1979) definition of minor and severe violence. A person was classified as engaging in *minor* aggression if he or she engaged in actions of threatening to hit;

Table 3.1   Physically Abusive Behaviors Reported by the Women

	Enacted by the Man	*Enacted by the Woman*
Threatened to hit or throw something at you	9.9	4.7
Threw, smashed, or kicked something	28.5	2.7
Threw something at you	8.7	1.1
Pushed, grabbed, or shoved you	24.5	9.7
Slapped you on the face	2.5	0.7
Slapped you on the body	11.3	10.3
Kicked, bit, or hit with a fist	10.2	6.0
Hit or tried to hit you with an object	1.0	0.9
Choked you	0.6	0.0
Beat you up	5.8	0.0
Threatened you with, or used, a knife or gun	1.0	0.0

NOTE: $N = 20$.

throwing, smashing, or kicking something; or pushing, grabbing, and shoving. *Moderate* aggression was defined as between one and five incidents of kicking, biting, hitting with a fist, hitting with an object, or choking. *Severe* aggression included six or more incidents of kicking, biting, hitting with a fist, hitting with an object, or choking; or as one or more incidents of beating or threatening with a weapon or using a weapon.

For the male-only aggressive relationships, two were classified as enacting minor aggression, three enacted moderate aggression, and five enacted severe aggression. The mutually aggressive relationships were broken down by whether the man's violence was more frequent/severe ($n = 6$), the woman's was more frequent/severe ($n = 2$), or the partners' were equally frequent/severe ($n = 2$). Within the mutually aggressive relationships, there were four classified as having contained severe aggression, with the man being the more frequent and severely aggressive partner. However, three of these relationships could be reclassified as male-only, given that the female partners' only act of aggression was to push their partners back one time.

Overall, in this sample of women, the man's use of aggression was both more severe and frequent than the woman's use of aggression.

Table 3.2   Classifications of Physical Aggression

	Minor Aggression[a]	Moderate Aggression[b]	Severe Aggression[c]
Male only aggressor	2	3	5
Both used aggression; male's use more frequent/severe	0	2	4
Both used aggression; female's use more frequent/severe	0	2	0
Both used aggression; both partners' use equal in frequency/severity	0	2	0

NOTE: $N = 20$.
a. Limited to threatening to hit; throwing or smashing or kicking something; or pushing, grabbing, and shoving.
b. Limited to between one and five incidents of kicking, biting, hitting with a fist, hitting with an object, or choking.
c. More than six incidents of kicking, biting, hitting with an object, hitting with a fist, or choking; or one or more incidents of beating or threatening with a weapon or using a weapon.

As a result, the women reported a variety of injuries, ranging from bruises and soreness to broken ribs and a fractured jaw. Finally, in all but one case, the women reported that the male partner was always the initiator of the aggressive behavior.

❧ The Relational Dynamics of Physical Aggression

The relational dynamics of physical aggression are not easy to describe succinctly. As the women relayed their stories of the progression of the abuse and their subsequent struggle to understand what had happened and why, an interwoven dynamic of jealousy, bickering, aggression, and control emerged. We have broken these dynamics into four sections: catalysts, communication dynamics, responding to his aggression, and the aftermath of an abusive episode. This breakdown is somewhat artificial in its implied linearity, because, as the women described their experiences, their stories were told in a more interconnected fashion. As so eloquently stated by Kirkwood (1993), the narratives were more circular as the women simultaneously described events, provided interpretations, commented on their thinking at the time of the abuse, and shared how their conceptions of what happened had changed over time.

Catalysts to Violence

Many authors have noted that "almost anything" can precipitate an abusive episode (Dutton & Golant, 1995; Laner, 1983; Lloyd & Emery, 1994; Makepeace, 1986; Stamp & Sabourin, 1995). This observation remains true in our data, as well; violence was precipitated by the woman engaging in a casual conversation with people waiting at a bus stop, wearing the "wrong" clothes or too much makeup, saying no to the man's sexual advances, an argument over drinking, and the woman's request to go home early, to name just a few.

The women's narratives reflected their attempts to try to understand what precipitated specific episodes of violence. Most of the time, the women easily described the immediate event or the moment in time that preceded his violence, reflecting a sense of searching out "What did I do?" and "How did this happen?" Thus, the seeds of self-blame started very early, as she searched her own actions for a clue to the "why." Even when the "reason" for his abusive behavior was invisible to her, it was clear that she still searched for an understanding of why violence had occurred:

> He said "Why do you say these things to me?" and I said "What things?" and I genuinely didn't know what I had said to upset him. We have talked about this in retrospect and he knows that I never did know what I had done wrong. So I kept saying "Please tell me what I did, please tell me," and he finally told me it was my joking about him sleeping on the couch. And then it just started off—there was no buildup—he just started off on a wild tangent and cursed and threw things and broke things until I cried.

Although the actual precipitating events varied a great deal from incident to incident and relationship to relationship, we did identify common catalysts to physical aggression. We use the term *catalyst* to refer to factors that surrounded or preceded the abusive episode and that the women described as underlying components or precursors to his abuse. The most consistently mentioned of these was a perceived threat to the relationship; other catalysts included stressful life events and alcohol or drug use.

Perceived Threats to the Relationship. The majority of the women (more than 70%) mentioned a perceived threat to the relationship as the primary catalyst for aggressive episodes. Our participants described many instances in which their interaction with other men or with friends sparked a jealous reaction in their partners that subsequently erupted into physical aggression. Sometimes this jealousy was manifested in his conviction that she was dating or sleeping with other men:

> He came by at all hours of the night in his car to make sure no one else's car was there by mine. He would call at 1 or 2 in the morning and say "Who's there with you?" and I'd say "I'm by myself" and he'd say "No you aren't" and then threaten to come over.

At times, relatively innocuous behavior, such as talking with an unknown man, precipitated the sense of threat and the subsequent abuse:

> I was waiting for him to pick me up in front of school. I was befriended by some guys and we struck up a conversation. When my boyfriend picked me up he didn't say anything. When we got home, physical violence occurred for the first time in our relationship. I had no idea it was coming. He caught me on the jaw and hit me up against the wall. I couldn't cry or scream or anything—all I could do was look at him. He picked me up and threw me against the wall and then started yelling and screaming at me that he didn't want me talking to other guys.

> [Once] a lot of construction workers whistled and said things to me as we were walking by. [My boyfriend] wouldn't take it out on them. Instead, he hit me around when we got to the car.

Perceived threats extended well beyond the fear of her interacting with other men; the threats included her interaction with female friends:

> [The first time he was aggressive] was when a bunch of my girlfriends
> had all gone away to school and were back for Thanksgiving and I was
> with them and he wanted me to be with him. . . . When I did things with
> other people and not with him, that's when I could tell.

The threats also sprang from jealousy over her career goals and her
very happiness:

> I was playing basketball and I was active and I was going places and
> doing things. . . . And he hated his job. I think that's another thing. Here
> I came home and enjoyed my day, and he hated his job, and was just
> jealous of my happiness.

Finally, several women also noted incidents wherein their own
jealousy was the precipitator of an aggressive episode:

> At a party he was sitting on a bed with his former girlfriend and I
> thought something was happening and he never told me for sure. He
> got mad and I got mad and he told me to leave. But, when I tried to leave
> he wouldn't let me and he got in the car with me and I don't know what
> happened but I had bruises all over.

> Well, it was the same through the whole thing. He cheated on me, I
> found out about it, and I wanted to know, and . . . I'd confront him. And
> he would go off.

In part, the theme of regulating emotional distance in the relationship runs throughout these anecdotes; when he perceives that she is
disloyal to the relationship, or when she questions his relational actions, violence may erupt. Ferraro (1988) and Sugarman and Hotaling
(1989) described the dynamic that underlies such jealousy as em-
bodying a threat to the man's sense of self and as a violation of his
need for loyalty. Dutton (1988) and Dutton and Browning (1988) described the dynamic in terms of a fear of abandonment. Certainly, the
vignettes provided previously illustrate a similar dynamic of a perceived violation of a "loyalty ethic" in these premarital relationships.
What is so striking about the women's narratives is how clearly they
parallel the stories told by severely battered women of the extreme
jealousy of their husbands (Dobash & Dobash, 1979; Dutton, 1988;
Dutton & Golant, 1995; Kirkwood, 1993; NiCarthy, 1987). It is chill-

ing to hear the possible precursors of severe battering and control reflected in these young women's descriptions of their intimate relationships during their teenage and young adult years.

Stressful Life Events. About 20% of the women in this sample linked stressful life events to their boyfriends' use of physical aggression. The role of such stress has been well documented in the literature on courtship violence (see, e.g., Makepeace, 1983; Marshall & Rose, 1987; Mason & Blankenship, 1987). Our participants described a sophisticated understanding of the link between stress and aggression, for the presence of stressful events per se was not spoken of as a simple cause of aggression. Rather, the women described how they became the scapegoat of the stress:

> Anything that went wrong or that he didn't like, he'd get very upset. School, football, family—it would carry over to me. I was a scapegoat—someone he could run to and take it out more or less on me.

The women also described how the stress served as a form of pressure on their boyfriends:

> His mom was really pushing us to stay together, because she really liked me, and so I am sure that was extra pressure on him.

> It may have been the pressure he was on with the coaches. Get up and run, go to class, practice, lift weights sometimes, homework, etc. . . . Maybe that, school and trying to party. Their day is completely planned and they don't get to choose anything.

The women described the ways in which his aggression was a response to a series of stressful life events that were happening all around him:

> The actual abuse didn't happen until the last year we dated, and I think it happened because his mother and father were going through a divorce. They had been divorced and remarried, and now they were going through a [second] separation. . . . I think it was a lot of aggression on his part as to what was happening around him. The father had set fire to the house and burned it down. [My boyfriend] had bought me a ring, and the father got some things out of the house, and the ring was one, and the father sold it.

Thus, stressful life events were portrayed as having a complex link to the use of violence. It was not a particular life event per se; rather, it was a web of events and pressures that was related both to his being upset and to his use of violence.

Alcohol and Drug Use. Alcohol and drug use were mentioned as a catalytic factor by about one third (35%) of the women. As with stress, the role of alcohol in physical aggression has been well documented (Leonard, 1999). Alcohol played multiple roles as a catalyst; some participants saw it as one of a series of factors that surrounded his use of violence:

> I found out he was cheating on me, so about 1 in the morning I went storming into his house, and he was in bed. He had been drinking and smoking pot and all he wanted to do was go to sleep. I was pretty mad and I wanted to know right then what was going on. I just aggravated and aggravated him until he finally just got up and threw some furniture around and picked me up by my jacket and was shaking me around and cussing me out and telling me to leave him alone and I was terrified. I sat down and bawled because it scared me to death.

Only one participant noted that alcohol was always associated with aggression; she believed that alcohol was the primary cause of his abusive behavior, and that his personality would change from Jekyll to Hyde when he drank:

> He would drink and it would be like he would totally change personalities on me. . . . He was so nice when he wasn't drinking. . . . He was just perfect, a very loving person. As soon as he would drink it would be like a switch. It hurt me really bad.

> Alcohol was also portrayed as an indication of underlying unhappiness or difficulty dealing with life: "He was always unhappy and when he'd drink, he'd get worse. It was like he wanted to get into trouble. He wanted to get caught doing something—he wanted to go to jail."

Again, the women did not speak of alcohol and drug use as a unitary catalyst, but rather as one of the myriad factors that served to catalyze his lashing out with physical aggression.

Communication Dynamics

As we noted in Chapter 2, our framework for examining physical aggression in courtship encompasses the conceptualization of aggression as a communicative act. As a result, when we examined the women's narratives, we were very interested in the interpersonal dynamics that characterized the overall relationship between perpetrator and victim as well as the patterns of communication and conflict that preceded the eruption of aggression.

Within the narratives provided by the women we interviewed, physical aggression often was embedded in an argument or conflict:

> I remember one time when we lived in the dorms we got into a fight or something . . . and I slammed his door and it made him mad, so he got a stick out of his car and was coming over toward me. . . . [Another time] I don't know what we were arguing about but I remember he took a chair and slammed it to the floor and crushed it all to pieces.

> We bickered a lot and he would hit things, throw you know. . . . He wanted to keep it away from me but you know it just ended up being toward me.

The women described these and many other episodes of conflict that escalated in intensity and anger and resulted in physical aggression. Their descriptions are in keeping with previous research that has emphasized the role of physical aggression as a conflict negotiation strategy that is enacted when other strategies have failed and the conflict has escalated out of control (Lloyd & Emery, 1994; Stets, 1992). For some of the women, the association between a heated disagreement and violence became so "predictable" that they attempted to avoid conflict or angering their partners altogether:

> After the first time it happened, I tried to walk on eggshells, but after that, arguments just happened.

> I knew that things could upset him. I remember that we'd write notes back and forth at school and if a sentence wasn't phrased just right and he took it wrong we'd get into an argument. . . . I noticed that he got upset very easy so I tried to do things so he wouldn't get upset.

Most of the women (70%) noted that ineffective communication patterns were part of the dynamic of his use of aggression. These ineffective patterns included an inability to talk about feelings without escalation into anger:

> We never communicated about feelings. He never said, "I'm mad." He just showed me.

> If I just wanted to sit down and talk about our relationship or anything, he doesn't really know how to sit down and talk, without getting upset. . . . He starts getting upset and his voice starts getting loud.

The patterns also included an unwillingness to talk over some issues at all:

> There was no discussing with me, he'd just say, "Christmas, I'm not being with you, I'm going out with my friends." He didn't care about my feelings.

> I'll ask "What's wrong?" and he'll treat me like shit and I'll just yell back, "You can't treat me this way" . . . and then he shuts me off—he'll stop talking to me like I don't exist.

> I am not much of an arguer, I don't like to fight. . . . I have a lot of anger and don't know how to deal with it—I guess I deal with it by trying to avoid it—I don't want to deal with it constructively.

Finally, there were instances of verbal abuse and emotional coercion:

> He'd hit things, like he'd hit the cabinet or something . . . but then you know then it was just real hateful, deceitful, verbal stuff and then if he'd thrown something or you know he'd just smack me or hit me.

> He would hurt me verbally too . . . called me a bitch.

> He would start calling me names like whore and stuff like that and saying that all I wanted was the male part of the man—that's what he was saying all the time. He would say it in front of people and it was really embarrassing.

He had a knife that he carried all the time that he could get out and be playing with it right by my face or stick it underneath my chin and say, "Well, I might as well just get this over with." He'd do it with such an attitude that you would think he was kidding about it.

He also gave me a lot of psychological stuff. Like, telling, just telling me things, like "I'm the only person that's good for you" and so on. Just a lot of terrible things. It made me think, maybe he is the only guy that will ask me out or go out with me.

Some of the women (25%) also described a dynamic of high volatility. This was described in terms of blowing up and exploding:

He'd just blow up and I'd figure out afterwards why he'd do it. He would never talk calmly when he was mad or in an argument—he'd just explode.

I could see it coming, he was like a time bomb. He was just building, ready to explode. I could tell by his actions from just sitting and making fists or get real restless and get blood red. His voice could tell me that he was getting angrier by the minute.

The women described the high volatility in terms of anger:

He'd never touch me unless he was angry, unless he was totally out of control mad. Always it happened in the hottest moment of anger.

Throwing things was a way of venting his anger. He wasn't rationalizing what he was doing. It was more of a spontaneous action. It was do and then think.

Previous research on the dynamics of physical aggression in courting and dating relationships corroborates the descriptions provided by our participants. Many researchers noted the embeddedness of aggression in conflict interaction that is negative, blaming, hostile, verbally aggressive, coercive, and attacking (Bird et al., 1991; Gryl et al., 1991; Infante et al., 1989; Lloyd, 1999; Riggs, 1993; Riggs & O'Leary, 1996; Ronfeldt et al., 1998; Spitzberg, 1997).

The narratives also support conceptualizations that note the volatile and expressive nature of physical aggression (e.g., Spitzberg, 1997; Stets, 1988). However, only a subset of the women (25%) described volatility/expressiveness as a dynamic of the aggression they had experienced. This is an important issue in the debate about whether violence is expressive or instrumental. From the narratives we analyzed for this book, and based on our other work on domestic violence (e.g., Lloyd, 1999), we have concluded that, for some men, physical aggression is both expressive and instrumental, and for some it is largely instrumental alone. As seen in a later section of this chapter, this conclusion stems in part from our discovery that every woman we interviewed spoke of the underlying dynamic of control.

Responding to His Aggression

In this section, we address how the women responded in the short run to the physical abuse they experienced. We discuss the initial reactions of disbelief and fear and the dynamics surrounding whether the young women fought back and responded to the men's violence with violence of their own.

The first time that physical violence occurred in the relationship, most of the women responded with a sense of disbelief. They used phrases such as "I wouldn't believe that it was happening" or "I was dumbfounded" in describing their reactions. It was clear that for many of the women, the abuse literally caught them by surprise; at least the first time, it was a totally unexpected occurrence in their relationship. For those young women whose partners promised never to hit again, that sense of horror and surprise was revisited each time this promise was broken. As we see subsequently in the section addressing this sense of disbelief, the "unreality" of the abuse contributed in important ways to the meaning-making process as these young women reflected on the abuse and attempted to make sense out of what had happened to them and to their relationships.

The other predominant reaction to the violence they experienced was fear. Most of the young women described their immediate reactions in terms of being scared, frightened, and emotionally distraught:

> The violence scared me very bad. When he would throw things I was shaking and crying, He would be walking around and I was sitting on the couch afraid to get in the line of fire. The last time when he put his fist through the briefcase I left the room and went to my bedroom and

closed the door, I was crying and he was calling me. Finally, I got up enough courage to go in there, but I was very slow in going in because I was trying to prepare myself in case he started doing it again. I wanted to be able to get out.

Scary! I mean, I would cry and stuff, and I kept wanting him to tell me that it wouldn't happen again. . . . I'd just sit in my room being scared and cry.

This fear was also the primary reason that 50% of the women did not retaliate with physical aggression of their own. For example, one young woman responded to our question "Why didn't you hit back?" by stating:

Because I was scared that if I hit him back, he'd hit me three times harder than he did. If he gets into one of those moods, the best thing to do is let him do whatever he wants to and just get away from him. (Emery & Lloyd, 1994, p. 253)

Other women acknowledged that they wanted to hit back, but fear kept them from doing so:

I wanted to [hit him back] but I was afraid to. . . . He was 6'4", weighed 250 pounds. He was huge. (Emery & Lloyd, 1994, p. 254)

[I was] scared to. I was afraid he'd fight back and it would be worse. I raised my hand several times to hit him and he warned me not to.

There was one additional reason for behaving nonviolently in the face of his violence; for 2 women, it reflected their core values of not behaving violently:

I never hit him back. That's not the way I vent my anger. I verbalize or hold it back until later. I was taught differently to vent anger.

On the other hand, despite these feelings of fright and disbelief when he behaved with violence, 50% of the young women fought back with physical violence of their own. However, the physical aggression used by the women was both qualitatively and quantitatively different from the physical aggression used by the men.

First, in all but one case among the women who were aggressive, the male partner was the one who usually initiated physical aggression. Second, the women's enactment of aggression was less frequent than the men's violence, a finding that is not in keeping with the results of most larger quantitative studies of courtship violence (Spitzberg, 1997; Sugarman & Hotaling, 1989). Third, the women's aggression was clearly less severe than the men's aggression; her aggression was qualitatively different from his, and, in some cases, not even taken seriously by the man:

> If he hit me, I'd be mad at him, and I figured if you hit me, I'm going to hit you back. So I would just, he would just laugh about it. My hits wouldn't compare with his and he says laughing "Can't you hit any harder than that?" or something like that. I was just trying to pay him back for hitting me.

> He was just really hateful and malicious in his verbal stuff, and I'm really sensitive to stuff like that and I couldn't think . . . I couldn't think of what to say back at him and so that's when I would throw back a pencil or something. (Emery & Lloyd, 1994, p. 256)

Why did half of the women "hit back"? In Emery and Lloyd (1994), we noted that the reasons women provided for hitting back were very complex—much more complex than the reasons for refraining from responding with violence. Furthermore, the women's explanations for why they hit back went deeper than the usual explanation of self-defense or self-protection, to encompass a sense of fighting for one's very "self." We found two major themes emerging: her violence as an attempt to establish a balance of control in the relationship, and her violence emanating from frustration and anger (Emery & Lloyd, 1994).

Violence as an attempt to establish balance in the relationship encompassed several issues. To some extent, it was an attempt to literally stop his abuse, yet at the same time it could represent regaining control over one's self or one's life. Both of these issues are apparent in the following narrative:

> [I hit back] to show him that he was not going to beat me up, that he was not going to hurt me, because I was going to hurt him right back. To let

him know what he was doing to me. . . . It was my way too, of saying, "Hey, I'm not this little girl you think you're going to control, because I am not going to let you." And so I'd hit him back, trying to get away from him. (Emery & Lloyd, 1994, p. 254)

The term *resistance* is most applicable in those cases in which the woman's use of violence is in response to her partner's attempts to hold dominance over her. One young woman was particularly eloquent on this point:

I think that he thinks that because he's the guy I should listen and do what he says. Which I don't agree with. Just like the time he thought that it was all right to aggravate me [tease, pinch, hit playfully], and when I told him to quit it, he just wasn't taking me seriously. And he thought that because he was the guy, he should be able to do whatever he wanted to do. . . . I was just trying to pay him back for hitting me. (Emery & Lloyd, 1994, p. 254)

Although these narratives do contain some elements of retaliation and self-defense, they do not stop there. Rather, they contain multiple meanings of resistance and regaining control. It should be noted that the women talked of resisting not only the violence but also the myriad forms of his attempts to control with whom they interacted, what they wore, what they would do as a couple, and so forth. The women's descriptions of why they used violence often were contextualized within a narrative of the many ways men enacted power and dominance over the women. As in the work of Umberson et al. (1998), experiencing violence had a significant negative effect on the sense of personal control these women felt.

The other recurrent theme underlying women's reasons for responding to violence with violence was frustration and anger. Sometimes, the frustration resulted from the partner's use of nonresponsiveness as a form of control:

Usually I fight back, but it's pointless, because it's the same result. Usually I'll ask what's wrong and he'll treat me like shit and I'll just yell back "You can't treat me this way and I'm not going to stay in a relationship like this." . . . And then he shuts me off, he'll stop talking to me like I don't exist and that's when I start throwing things.

Other times, it was his badgering and blaming that was high-lighted as the reason behind her use of violence:

> I would just get so aggravated and frustrated because he would just turn everything around and blame it on me. And I knew it wasn't my fault, but he would just keep on, keep on, keep on, and on, and on, and on. (Emery & Lloyd, 1994, p. 256)

Also, her violence was a result of not being able to express thoughts verbally when in the heat of anger:

> I guess that it's just that I can't say enough to make my point when I'm mad, so I'll just have to punch him, I guess, I don't know. . . . I think it almost actually reflects . . . just jolting out my anger, instead of saying it or stuff.

Although at first glance her use of violence appears to exactly paral-lel his use of violence (both describe controlling and expressive as-pects of physical violence), both Campbell (1993) and Emery and Lloyd (1994) argued that the instrumental aspects of violence are con-textually very different for men and women. For example, although battering men describe a control dynamic that encompasses their need to dominate women or to force women into adopting their rules for the relationship, these men do not frame their use of aggression in terms of responding to a woman's extreme attempts to control them (Barnett & LaViolette, 1993; Campbell, 1993; Dutton & Golant, 1995; Emery & Lloyd, 1994; Umberson et al., 1998).

These results are also very supportive of the work of Coan et al. (1997) and Jacobson et al. (1994). These authors noted that fear and resistance are responses that go hand in hand for women who have been battered by their husbands. Rather than being beaten down by the battering, the women they studied made attempts to resist the domination, control, and violence of their husbands. Simultaneously, they expressed extreme fear of their husbands, knowing that batter-ing could happen again. Our sample of women in courting relation-ships exhibited very similar reactions, on the one hand relaying how frightened they were of men's violence and on the other hand talking about fighting back, and fighting to regain their sense of autonomy and control over their lives.

The Aftermath of Aggression

Our final word in this section on the relational dynamics of physical aggression has to do with what happened after the incident of aggression. The aftermath of aggression was succinctly described by the women as going in one of two directions. On the one hand, some of the men acted as if nothing had happened:

> The next morning after he broke the door down he acted like nothing had ever happened.

> I was waiting for him to say something about [the violence], anything, and he just came in and went to sleep. He saw what I looked like [her face was bruised] and he didn't ask.

> I told him not to ever hit me like that again, or I wouldn't be around. . . . I don't think he took me seriously, because he was just laid on the couch and acted like he was watching television. . . . His face was staring straight at the television screen.

On the other hand, some of the men apologized profusely for having lost control and behaving aggressively. Like those whose descriptions Walker (1979) provided, these men would beg the women's forgiveness and promise never to transgress again:

> He said he was sorry and cried and asked me not to break up with him. At this time, I didn't know about all the studies that said of course it would happen again. I let myself believe him, because I was really vulnerable and away from my parents at college and trying to do well.

> He sat down and cried and said "I am sorry I lost control." I said "Never again, you can leave." He just apologized over and over again.

> He promised that it would never happen again. But of course we know that it did.

> When he's finished then he's sorry and he cries and he says "I'm just so afraid that you're going to leave me and this will be the last time that I'll see you and I just don't know what to do and I just have to know that you love me."

However, these apologies did not always come unencumbered. At times, the apologies were merely a precursor to blaming the aggression on the woman:

> He'd always say "I'm so sorry!" But, he always had to add the words, "but if you hadn't made me so mad, I wouldn't do it." And I would say, "Well, it doesn't matter what I do, you should never hit a person," and he would say, "Well, you shouldn't make me so mad." He was sorry on one hand, but justify it because it was my fault—that I caused it.

As can be seen in the section of this chapter titled "Constructing Meaning Around the Experience of Physical Aggression," this latter dynamic is an important one to examine, for it speaks to one of the many ways that men divest themselves of responsibility for their use of aggression and blame it on women.

❧ The Dynamics of Control

In Chapter 2, we discussed our conceptualization of physical aggression as a tactic of coercive control of women. Many researchers have noted the underlying aspect of control, commenting on violence as a way of causing fear, forcing compliance, intimidating, punishing for a perceived transgression, gaining domination, and/or forcing her to stay in the relationship (Dutton & Golant, 1995; Emery & Lloyd, 1994; Goldner et al., 1990; Kirkwood, 1993; Marshall, 1994; Ptacek, 1988; Stets, 1988). As noted in our framework, both our feminist and relational influences led us to be particularly interested in the ways in which the women we interviewed framed physical aggression as a tactic of control.

One of the most interesting results of our interviews with the young women who had experienced physical aggression during courtship is that every respondent spoke about the dynamics of control at some point during the interview. Often, their descriptions of control came in response to our question "What do you think he hoped to accomplish? In other words, why did he hit you?" Other facets of control emerged as the women described the first or latest incident of abuse and as they described their relationships overall.

Aggression as a tactic of control was not discussed by the women as a "unitary" phenomenon. In two important ways, the women gave very complex explanations for "why he hits." First, their explanations did not speak singularly of control but rather spoke of a spiraling complex of factors that both catalyzed his aggression and explained his behavior after the fact. The most consistent explanation revolved around his need for control, which clearly placed responsibility on the aggressor. Ironically, however, the women also constructed complex explanations that served to excuse his behavior and place blame on themselves (this dynamic is discussed extensively in the subsequent section titled "Constructing Meaning Around the Experience of Physical Aggression").

Second, the women provided many nuanced descriptions of men's control of them and of the course of the relationship. Control as they described it was a multifaceted phenomenon, ranging from domination of the course of an argument to the male right to "whip her into shape" to literal physical control that prevented her leaving the relationship. Previously, we addressed how the perceived threat to the relationship served as a key catalyst to an aggressive episode. Our discussion of control ideally illuminates the dynamics that underlie such perceived threats.

Our analysis revealed four interrelated facets of control: domination of an argument, domination of the woman and the relationship, keeping her in the relationship, and ownership and extreme control of her person. These four facets are not entirely distinct but are interconnected, for multiple facets were often described by a woman as she delineated the web of a man's control over everything from her feelings to the people with whom she interacted.

Domination of an Argument

In talking about why their male partners hit them, the women described many instances in which the violence emanated from the men's attempts to dominate the course of a particular argument. At the most basic level, the women described the ways in which their partners' use of physical violence was an attempt to "make us listen":

> [He would hit me] to get me to listen to him. To get me to see his vantage point or way of thinking or to get some sense into me, is what he'd tell me. To get his point across and the only way he could do it was with force.

The men also used violence to prove they were right:

> I think he just wanted to be more powerful. He wanted me to see that he was right.

At times, this type of domination of an argument was enacted when she stood her ground or would not do what he wanted:

> Well, the pattern would start when we would get in an argument or something and we'd each have one side of the argument, and if he was right—if he thought he was right—and I'd be sitting there arguing, I'd go "NO" and if I stood my ground, and I refused to see what he was saying, and if he stood his ground, it would get worse . . . and most of the time I would end up . . . saying "I'm wrong" even though I thought something else just to get the argument over. He kept saying "I'm going to make you." So he'd pin me down or he'd put me down. Or if I tried to get away, you know, he'd do stuff to me. . . . He'd hold me down or grab me or pull me or throw me in the car.

These narratives once again illustrate how aggression was embedded within conflict interaction—indeed, aggression can quite literally serve as a means for "winning" during an argument or for getting one's way (Lloyd & Emery, 1994). They also illustrate how domination of those arguments was highly important to some of the men who were abusive, and the ways in which that domination can serve as a means of rejecting female influence (Coan et al., 1997).

Domination of the Woman and the Relationship

Domination clearly did not stop with controlling a particular argument but extended to the domination of the woman and the relationship, as well. Here, the women described a complicated dynamic, which included his greater power in the relationship and a sense that he believed he had the right to tell her what to do as well as the right to mold her to conform to his idealized image of a romantic partner.

For some, this domination was apparent in who made decisions about where to go, what to do, and even how she should dress:

> We did what he wanted. Eat, buy, see what he wanted. I found myself wearing clothes I would of never chosen, but that's what he wanted. . . . If he wanted something, it was just automatic. I was scared to object, or he'd be abusive.

> It would be like we were just sitting around. . . . Like if he would want me to do something and I wouldn't want to do it, he might would threaten or like if I wanted him to go do something with me and he didn't want to then he might shove me and say "Get out of my way."

For others, it was an attempt to bend her will to his:

> [He would hit me] to show he was dominant over me. . . . I never felt he was going to pin me down and beat the pulp out of me because it wasn't like that. It was more like you're going to do what I say.

> [He was] very overbearing, very commanding, "Yes you will."

One woman even used that language of "obey me" in describing her partner's domineering behavior, language that seems particularly ironic given that our courting relationships are so often construed as romantic and egalitarian:

> He was extremely domineering, he wanted me to be at his beck and call, "Don't betray me and don't lie to me." Obey me kind of a father thing, do as I say not as I do kind of thing.

Ultimately, controlling the woman also meant controlling her feelings, her self-confidence, and even her mind:

> He had total control of my feelings—everything—he'd tell me when to cry and when to feel sad.

> He'd try and control me and beat down my self confidence. . . . He set it up to be there when I was down.

> He would start saying things that—he would try to change to where it looked like it would be my fault—he would turn the tables and it would be like he was trying to control my mind.

In other instances, the domination of her and the relationship embodied aspects of trying to change her in a multitude of ways, from wanting her to be more perfect to wanting her to change her very essence:

> He thought that by hitting me he could "whip me into shape." He is a perfectionist—everything he does is perfect. . . . He felt that I could do better in some things.

> [After the violent episode] we'd make up and it would just go away. But down deep though, it bothered me. Because he was just wanting me to change so much, and I refused and can't do that.

Ironically, in some cases he also wanted to change her back into the more dependent person she had been at the beginning of the relationship:

> He talked down to me a lot. It was like, you know, he wanted me to be the little girl I'd been when he'd started dating me. A little girl that said, "OK, whatever," and gave in to whatever he said without fighting about it, and who said "OK, you know everything and I know nothing." . . . He told me I was selfish, stubborn, immature, and I couldn't handle life without him. He wouldn't let me wear skirts, and I had to button everything all the way up. . . . I wore my hair a certain way. . . . He was always trying to tell me what to do.

Some of the women discussed this facet of control as grounded in male socialization. One woman eloquently described her partner's need to control the relationship and provided an explanation for that need that was based on the milieu in which he had been raised:

> He thought it was OK to hit a female. That he had to have the upper hand at all times. That he had to be the controlling figure in the relationship. . . . He grew up in a country town where the mom is supposed to be the barefoot and pregnant type woman, the man is supposed to go out and make a living and be the one who is controlling. That's the way he thought things were supposed to be.

Another women described his domination of her and of the relationship as part and parcel of "proving he was a man":

He used to say "This is the way it's going to be." That's his way of proving he was a man, and that was where his dominance [was] over me, his
fear over me because I made just as much money.

Keeping Her in the Relationship

The previous section delineates some of the ways that the men use
physical and psychological coercion to control their partners and relationships. The ultimate in the domination of the relationship is seen in
the women's descriptions of what happened when they tried to leave
the scene of an argument or leave the relationship. At times, physical
restraint was used quite literally to keep a woman from leaving:

> He'd never let me leave the house . . . maybe because he was so insecure
> that he thought if I left the house that I would never come back again.
> Sometimes he would stand in the door and keep me from leaving.

> I was just trying to leave and he'd pinned me down. . . . . He was just
> showing me he wanted me around. But he really wanted me to . . . stay
> there, because I kept saying I'm leaving and he kept stopping me.

> I was packing up my things—I told him I was going to leave if he was
> going to continue to drink—I was walking by the door and he grabbed
> me with his arm around my neck. I fell to the floor and he dragged me
> into the bedroom and punched on my face. I was crying and screaming
> and I got scared 'cause he wouldn't stop and he kept on continually hit-
> ting me.

At other times, psychological constraint was sufficient, when the
fear of what would happen when she attempted to leave served to
keep her in the relationship longer than she desired. One participant even noted the heightened risk that she felt as she contemplated leaving her abusive partner:

> I tried to break up "cold turkey" but you can't do that in an abusive rela-
> tionship because that makes them madder and more violent.

Finally, keeping her in the relationship meant that her independence had to be restrained as well:

> He wouldn't let me have a car because he didn't want me to go out or I would meet someone and leave him or become too independent.... He didn't want to give me too much freedom that I would leave him.

An interesting duality emerged in some of the narratives. On the one hand, he would beg her to stay and proclaimed that she was the best thing that ever happened to him. On the other hand, he would make her show her love and concern by staying in spite of his coercive behavior:

> Part of the violence from his point of view was pushing me to the point of view where I lost it. He believed if he pushed me to the edge—pushed all my buttons until I lost it—and still not leave—if he could push me to the limit and I stayed—that meant I loved him.

Ultimately, dominance and aggression were tangled up into a complicated web of trying to keep her close:

> [He hit me] to show he was dominant over me. [That] he could keep me in this relationship by doing that.

Three important dimensions are reflected in these anecdotes on the dynamics of keeping her in the relationship. First, the batterer's fear of abandonment (Dutton, 1988; Dutton & Browning, 1988) is echoed in the narratives of these women as they describe the ways that men's physical aggression literally and figuratively kept them in the relationship. Second, the heightened risk for women at the time of leaving an abusive partner (Barnett & LaViolette, 1993; Kirkwood, 1993; NiCarthy, 1987) is apparent, for this may be a time when the potential of women's leaving becomes real and perhaps the most emotionally enraging. Finally, the narratives on keeping her in the relationship presage the next facet of control: the perception of male rights of "ownership" of their dating partners.

Ownership and Extreme Control of Her Persona

In its more extreme forms, the domination of the woman and the relationship spilled over into a dynamic of male ownership of the woman's very persona. Once again, the women's narratives were reminiscent of descriptions provided by battered women of the extremes of control that battering husbands use; what is so chilling here is the realization of how very early in the development of these relationships that ownership rights and possessiveness were established. All too often, this dynamic arose after less than a year of dating.

The women we interviewed were eloquent in their descriptions of the dynamics of ownership. One woman described an incident in which, after another man grabbed her arm on a dance floor, her boyfriend declared "Don't touch her, she's mine." Others described similar incidents of possessiveness and property rights:

> It was like I was his. I didn't look at other guys, I didn't speak unless spoken to. I should know his mind and know when to fix dinner, what clothes he was going to wear. I should be his slave—his servant. I was his property, and I had no use except making his life more easy.

> When he first started to be possessive, I thought it was kind of neat. This guy must really like me to be that obsessive. But then it got to be obsessive possessive—it was like I was just something to own, like a car or something.

Once again, a perceived threat of the presence of a rival (even the hypothetical rival of the future) was enough to trigger the dynamic of ownership and abuse:

> I made a comment that if anything happened to him [her boyfriend], anyone else would be able to tell that I wasn't a virgin. And he leaned across the table and grabbed my hair and pulled me out by it to the truck. . . . He said I should never say anything like that, that nothing's going to happen, and no one would ever want me and that he is the one for me. . . . It was very fragile to him, thinking that someone else would have me.

The most extreme examples of ownership came as some of the women described the lengths to which their boyfriends would go in checking up on them. These young women had to prove their loyalty constantly, as their boyfriends used any means possible to ensure that their "property" was safeguarded from the attention of others:

> I got a job in a paint store. . . . He checked on me six or more times a day. In 2 weeks I made manager and that upset him. He thought that the

owner of the store liked me, so he threw all my makeup away and wouldn't let me wear any.

He wanted to know where I was. If I didn't answer the phone on the second or third ring, I was in trouble. If I went shopping, anywhere, I had to have proof of where I was, time and everything.

Summary of the Dynamics of Control

The women we interviewed described the dynamics of control as multifunctional, with no one pattern or dynamic predominating. In some cases, aggression as a tactic of control was described mainly in terms of his attempts to control the course of an argument and to assert his rights over his partner's rights. This type of control dynamic parallels the dynamics outlined by Johnson (1995), as he described the goals of "common couple violence." In some ways, this control was the least insidious, in the sense that its origins were embedded mainly within conflict negotiation patterns. In other cases, the dynamics of control were more pervasive, for they covered not only arguing rights but also domination over what they did as a couple, when she was allowed to leave, and where she was allowed to go. In the most extreme forms, control dynamics included everything from ensuring that he won all arguments, to checking the mileage on her car, to punishing her with physical abuse every time another man even looked at her. Clearly, in such relationships, forms of "patriarchal terrorism" (Johnson, 1995) already have been enacted.

The underlying dimensions of these facets of control bear scrutiny. We believe that two interlocked dimensions are at play here: the ethic of female loyalty to the relationship, and the assumptions inherent in male privilege. Here we build on Ferraro's (1988) observations that violations of the need for loyalty and the need for control are the two primary catalysts to violence for batterers. Certainly, loyalty is a strong theme that runs throughout the narratives on the dynamics of control and the narratives of jealousy. In more than one relationship, the men actively searched for evidence of their partners' disloyalty and, in the absence of hard evidence, constructed scenarios of betrayal from the women's interactions with other men, with friends, and with family. In other relationships, the fear of her leaving was palpable and served as the underlying reason for his violence. All too often, loyalty was taken to the extremes of possessiveness and ownership. It is important to ask why her actions were so often construed in terms of a perceived violation of loyalty to him. We speculate that it connects back to a discourse of relationships that emphasizes the overwhelming importance of relationships to women, a discourse that frames relationship health and quality as her responsibility, and, by corollary, frames relationship dysfunction as her fault.

The dynamics of control also reflect the discourse of male privilege and power. As the women relayed their stories of the dynamics surrounding physical violence, they unwittingly described a web of male domination of everything from the outcome of an argument to whether she could go out with friends. Such privilege may stem from his socialization into a male honor code that emphasizes his "right" to be the dominant partner in intimate relationships to maintain control by rejecting her influence and attempts to stand up for herself (Coan et al., 1997; Umberson et al., 1998). Unfortunately, the discourse of male privilege is rendered palatable by the discourse of equality (that way we do not have to recognize it) and reinforced by the discourse of romance (he is, after all, the knight in shining armor—he is supposed to take charge).

As a final note to our discussion of control, it is important to ask whether the women's narratives were imbued with attempts to save face and present their own behavior in the best light and make their boyfriends look bad. We think not. As we listened to the young women struggle with how to make sense of all that had happened in these abusive relationships, we did not note a tendency for the women to engage in lots of socially desirable responses. Rather, as they tried to relay what happened, understand why, and move toward recovery from these highly traumatic experiences, we heard in their narratives a great deal of self-blame and a search for understanding that reflected the dominant discourses of courtship and violence.

☙ Constructing Meaning Around the Experience of Physical Aggression

One important question that our analysis of the women's narratives addresses is how the women construct meaning around the physical and psychological abuse that they have experienced. Here, we are interested in how the survivor strives to attach meaning to this unexpected occurrence, and how she frames her explanations of the underlying causes. Given our emphasis in Chapter 2 on the discourse of courtship and the discourse of aggression, it should come as no surprise that we also examined the women's stories with an eye toward unpacking how the dominant discourses affect the explanations and meanings that are attached to violence during courtship. In our analyses, we identified three interrelated phases in the meaning-making process: disbelief and confusion, excusing and forgiving the aggressor, and the dynamics of blaming the victim. We conclude this section with a discussion of how reframing the abuse ultimately was an important step in leaving the abusive partner.

Disbelief and Confusion

As noted previously, the first time physical violence occurred in the relationship, the women were shocked and filled with a sense of disbelief:

> I just couldn't believe it. I just could not believe that it was him doing this. We had a great relationship. . . . I just could not believe it was him doing this to me.

> It surprised me, because I didn't think that he would do anything like that. It just, it just took me by surprise. I didn't know he was like that.

> [I was] shocked! I couldn't believe that . . . he was doing it to me, I thought that it would never happen.

Even in several cases in which the young woman acknowledged that she was aware of the man's violent temper or of his past violence toward others, she still expressed surprise when it happened to her:

> I knew that his violent temper was a part of his personality. For lack of a better expression, I feel he was a "Billy-Bad-Ass." I'd never heard of him hitting a girl. I never thought he'd do it to me. I was stunned!

This sense of unreality and disbelief was paralleled by a sense of confusion as to how to make sense out of the violent behavior and what it meant for the young woman and for the relationship:

> I didn't know what to do. I knew something was wrong, but I didn't know what to do. He'd say he was sorry afterwards, and then he'd say "Let's not talk about it anymore, it won't happen again." But it always seems to happen again, you know? And I know he loves me and I love him too. It's just a mess.

Confusion also was apparent as the young women talked about why they did not always define their partners' violence and psychological control as abusive behavior. Although most recognized that it was not usual or normal behavior, they stopped short of applying the label "abuse":

> I knew it wasn't normal but I didn't think it was abuse. . . . When I think of abuse, I think of somebody, you know, beating somebody up. Having black eyes and stuff.

> I did have blood and black and blue behind my ears. I probably had a couple of bruises, but I wasn't beaten up badly. I didn't have to go to the hospital or anything like that.

> I, not knowing how a relationship is supposed to work, I guess I thought it [the physical abuse] was kinda normal, not normal, but I didn't know.

Finally, even at the time of our interview, which for all but one woman was after the relationship had ended, the women talked about their ongoing attempts to try to make sense of the abuse they had experienced:

> I think it is important to find out why. . . . There's got to be a reason why he would do this, when the same thing said to me wouldn't cause me to lose my temper like that.

> He was really nice, and I mean a lot. He really worried about me, but I didn't think he would ever hurt me. I mean I look back now and can see what was going on, but I couldn't then. I didn't expect it to happen.

What do these anecdotes tell us about why the violence was such a confusing event for these young women? Clearly, they point in part to the unexpected nature of the abuse as a culprit: Physical aggression is not a part of the "script" for a relationship, and, therefore, when it happens, it is difficult to decipher, especially in terms of what it means for the couple's future. At the very least, teenagers and young adults believe that if abuse happens, it will precipitate the end of the relationship (Carlson, 1996).

When an unexpected event happens in the midst of an intimate relationship filled with love and romance, it is no wonder that the victim draws on the dominant discourse of courtship to believe him when he says it will never happen again. After all, as we noted in Chapter 2, the dominant discourse emphasizes that love and romance will conquer all and that courtship is characterized by equality between men and women. Certainly, many of the young women we interviewed talked about the love they felt for their partners and how confusing it was to experience violence in the midst of other positive and romantic interactions:

> I think that's probably the reason that I stayed with him. It was just like two different persons and I knew the other person was loving and I loved him very much.

> I was living with him and I just left everyone else alone. I thought, I thought that we could live happily ever after, live on love.

> He was really, really romantic. He'd give me things, and send flowers to me, and write romantic stuff, real mushy intense stuff, and he really was, he showered me with love. . . . That's what's so confusing about him, because I still have a lot of his letters, and things, and cards, and stuff. He's kind of a young Romeo. You know he'd give me all this stuff, and then the next day, he'd be like, he'd be so evil. Jealousy and hate, it's confusing.

We hypothesize that the confusion felt by these young women as they searched for a way to make sense out of what had occurred was a result in part of the fact that physical violence simply is not part of the dominant discourse on courtship. How could it be, for violence violates all notions of romance and egalitarianism. Instead of addressing the possibility of violence, the romantic and egalitarian veneer of courtship encourages intimate partners to "forgive and forget" negative behaviors.

However, because it is rather difficult to forget that she has been slapped, or bruised, or hit, or punched, or coerced, or controlled by someone who says he loves her, the victim of violence searches for the meaning and cause of the behavior she has experienced. Herein lies the influence of the discourse of violence: Her search for meaning is affected by the dominant discourses, which emphasize that the aggressor is really not to blame for his "loss of control" and that the victim played a role in "driving him to it."

Excusing the Aggressor

In one of the very early articles on courtship violence, Henton et al. (1983) noted the tendency for victims to forgive and externalize the violence they had experienced. This same tendency was noted in the narratives provided by the young women in our study. The women did not speak in the language of blame, that is, they did not emphasize that it was his "fault," and they did not condemn him. Rather, their language reflected the many ways that they were seeking understanding and providing explanations for his violence toward them. Although, as we noted previously, the women framed their responses to the question "why he hits" clearly in the language of control, they also provided a wide variety of explanations for his control and violence. Instead of blaming, they seemed to be on an almost desperate search for the underlying cause of his behavior. Ultimately, the causes they discussed reflected the predominant discourse that emphasizes that, even though he was controlling and physically violent, it was not really his fault after all.

The underlying reasons provided for his behavior varied from woman to woman. Some directly excused his behavior by emphasizing that he did not mean to hurt them and that he did not want to hit them:

> It took me a long time for me to realize what was going on, 'cause I thought that it was my fault. And there weren't that many [incidents of aggression] where he hurt me.

> He'd hit things like he'd hit the cabinet or something you know, he's hit something else 'cause you know he didn't want to hit me. But then you know . . . [he] just smacked me or hit me.

Some also excused his behavior by saying that he was experiencing a lot of situational and external pressure that made him lose control:

> When he shook me I told him "Don't push me around, I don't like it." He'd never done it before, I didn't think it was a big deal, it was situational.

> I don't know if it's football. He took steroids for a while. . . . His mom could always tell when he was taking steroids. . . . He'd always push his mother against the wall when he was on them.

Other explanations emphasized the role of mental health and self-esteem in producing his violent behavior. The young women would talk in terms of their boyfriends as having a problem, as being insecure, and as having a low self-concept:

> Sometimes I think he is insecure. I don't know if that would cause him to do that or not. But, I think he is insecure.

> He has a low self-concept, so that might be one of the reasons he took things out on me.

> I just thought he was a very upset and disturbed person. Which he was.

As we noted in the section on dynamics, some women commented on his "volatile personality." One woman was quite direct; she explained his violence in terms of being "sick":

> I know that he is sick. . . . Once he started therapy—he actually told the truth. He told her [the therapist] he had no control over his temper and that he abused me, and she told him he was sick.

Finally, his family background was often cited as playing a role in producing a young man who resorted to violence against the woman he loved:

> His father was very physically aggressive with his wife. . . . His father had spanked his wife with a belt and . . . then one time he had her up against the wall by her neck and threatening her. . . . He [her boyfriend] had a couple of problems because of his childhood and I justified it [his violence toward her] because of his childhood.

> [His] father was always verbally marking him down. Son felt he was treated as a hired hand and not a son. Verbally abused by family and not loved. I still try to get him to get help.

> 'Cause his father was a shit to everybody. He made his family constantly prove that they loved him by taking his shit . . . so when J wants to know he's loved, instead of walking across the room and giving me a hug, or asking "Do you love me?" . . . what he needs to know is that he can be the ultimate asshole and I still won't go—that means I have unconditional love for him.

Ultimately, explaining his violent and controlling behavior in terms of external pressures, self-esteem, or the intergenerational transmission of violence all served as ways to understand the underlying reasons for his behavior. These explanations also served inadvertently to excuse his negative behavior. Furthermore, as shown in the next section, excusing him was often accompanied by his own self-excuses and blaming of the woman for his violence.

The Dynamics of Blaming the Victim

The dynamics of blaming the victim are multifaceted. On the one hand, the aggressor excused his behavior and simultaneously held his partner responsible for provoking his violence. On the other hand, the woman spoke of her role in the dynamics of the abusive behavior and how, over time, she came to believe that, at least in part, the violence was her fault. Coupled with this dynamic of self- and other blame is the isolation of the woman from family and friends, which served to keep her from questioning her self-blame and reframing her understanding of his abuse.

Aggressors excused their violence in a variety of ways. The women reported that sometimes the excusing was framed in terms of "If you wouldn't have made me so mad I wouldn't hit you." The women were told that their actions caused his loss of temper, and that they started it by doing or saying the wrong thing during an argument:

> I showed him the handprints [bruises on her arms], he was just like, "Well, if you would just sit down . . . if you would have acted like an adult and sat there and listened so we could talk civilized, you wouldn't of had those handprints on your arms." It was like, you did them, I didn't do them.

> He would make me feel like it was totally my fault for being illogical and whatnot. I would end up feeling it was my fault and I'd have to . . . it would be held over my head for a few days, a few weeks. . . . I would end up feeling like the bad seed.

The men also excused their behavior by minimizing their actions. "I didn't hurt you" was a familiar refrain to some of the women:

> I told him I was not going out with him anymore, and he was on top of me, choking me and I couldn't breathe, and he hit my nose, and my nose was bleeding. I said "Look what you've done" and he said "I haven't done anything." And my nose was bleeding!

> He never thought he hurt me, never. He'd force me down and I'd say "You're hurting me" and he'd say "I'm not hurting you!" And I would kick back and stuff and he would tell me that "How can I hurt you if you are not hurting me?" . . . I guess like after this episode, there were just more and more of them, he just quit believing that he was hurting me, because I said it every time and it got redundant I guess.

The young women also blamed themselves. They took responsibility in a multitude of ways, noting that it was their fault for starting the fight:

> I'd feel guilty like I shouldn't have started a fight. He wouldn't of been mean to me, if I had not smarted off and just sat there like an adult.

They also blamed themselves for acting spitefully:

> I don't know, it's just that . . . he starts getting upset and his voice starts getting loud, and I'm a very spiteful person, very testy, and I guess I push him.

Finally, they took responsibility for being attracted to the wrong kind of guy:

> In the past I've always been attracted to controlling type guys.... [One of my boyfriends] didn't show me as much love and didn't act like he loved me as much as other guys I dated so that kinda—it was like a challenge in a weird way. For some reason I was attracted to guys who acted like they didn't care for me.

Although in reality the young women were not at fault for "causing" him to be violent, what is clear is that they did over time come to believe that they were to blame. Some of the young women came to believe him when he said it was "your fault" or "you deserved it":

> He'd try and blame it on me and say it was my fault. I started to believe all of it.

> Like when my ex-husband slapped me in the face I felt that that was deserved, that that was out of love. I knew that was the limit—I knew what I could say and I said that on purpose to make him mad and hurt him and that [the slapping] was deserved to me.

They even felt guilty for staying in the relationship and putting up with the violence:

> I don't know why in the world I was so vulnerable. I don't know why in the world I let it go on. I'm irritated at myself. . . . I'm embarrassed because I've known better. I must have been out in left field to put up with this.

Unfortunately, for many of the young women who shared their stories with us, there was little opportunity to reconstruct their understanding of violence or to question their self-blame, for they did not often share the details of the abusive experience with friends or family. Some feared the negative reaction of their parents, noting that "My parents would have killed him." Others noted that lack of support from their families contributed to them staying with their abusive partners:

> Probably, if I hadn't been so naive, if I had been closer to my parents, I probably wouldn't have done it [stayed with her abusive boyfriend].... I know that's the truth because I wasn't getting along with my father at the time and needed, I wanted some guidance, I did. And he [the boyfriend] gave it to me. ... It was just like he [the boyfriend] was my support, he was my guidance, he was my family! ... I think that if parents make a child feel secure, then they don't need it from a boyfriend.

Some of the young women did not want to ruin their parents' perfect image of their boyfriends or did not want their parents to know how "stupid" they were for being with a man who hurt them:

> My parents came to really like him. And when we broke up and everything, they still talk about him. ... But they don't know how really bad it got. They don't need to know. I'll never tell them [about the abuse], I don't want them to know how stupid I was.

One young woman noted that even though she told her mother about the abuse, her mother did not advise her to break off the relationship:

> I did tell her, I did tell her about slapping me on the leg, and she didn't like that too well. Because like I said, her and daddy, they never would do anything like that. That's not how I was brought up, and she didn't like it because she didn't want to see me being treated like that. But she didn't say not to see him anymore, or say you should quit seeing him.

In another example, the mother of one of the abusive boyfriends actually helped provide a reason for his abuse. Although this mother was trying to help the young woman understand where the abuse was coming from, she also helped construct a meaning that emphasized that it was not her son's fault:

> His mother told me that B used to be the nicest guy you could meet. But then he got mixed up with J [a former girlfriend], and the things she did to him made him like he is. He never used to be physically violent. ... His mother said it was her. All the trouble that he has been mixed up in was tied in to her.

Friends played a critical role as well. Some friends warned her and, as shown in the next section, were instrumental in helping her leave.

More often, the women talked about losing their friends, especially due to the men cutting the women off from social ties:

> [He told me] "Your friends are only running around with you because of who your parents are." I didn't have a high opinion of myself. . . . He wanted me to withdraw [from my friends], and would tell me that my friends really didn't like me. It wasn't drastic—we'd go to church and sit in the balcony rather than down with everyone, and I'd only attend church and not any of the other activities I always went to.

This active isolation from friends served a sinister dual purpose, for, in the absence of outside interaction, the physical and psychological effects of his violent behavior could go undetected, and her opportunities to talk with others who might reframe his behavior as abusive were severely constrained.

Ultimately, excusing the aggressor and blaming oneself for the violence may have served another purpose for these women who experienced violence. It could be that this dynamic helped provide a rationale for staying with the aggressor. If his behavior was construed as nonintentional or externally precipitated, and if she believed that she played a role in precipitating the aggression, it would allow her to believe that violence would not necessarily happen again, or that, at the very least, she could control his violence by being on her best behavior. Thus, the dissonance caused by violence in the midst of a loving and romantic relationship can be reduced, for if it really was not his fault, and if he really did not mean to hurt her, perhaps things could be repaired. In the absence of opportunity to reconstruct his behavior as abusive, this belief system would be able to continue unquestioned. Indeed, as the next section illustrates, opportunities for these young women to end these relationships often occurred when the women began to see their partners and the abusive behavior in a new light.

Reframing the Aggression and Leaving the Relationship

How did these young women reframe the meanings they had attached to physical abuse and finally end their relationships with these abusive men? The dynamic was one of beginning to see their partners, and their partners' use of physical aggression, in a different light. For some of the women, this change in perception was a gradual process, similar to the growing awareness that something was wrong, as described by Kirkwood (1993). As one woman said,

> It took a long time for me to realize what was going on, because I thought it was my fault.

For others, it was experienced more as a sudden "ah-ha" experience:

> I stuck with him because I thought he had problems and maybe I could help. . . . I thought I was going to be the big hero and save him from doing worse things to someone else. Sitting in church one day I decided it was stupid and I wasn't going to put up with it anymore.

Sometimes this sudden change in perception of the partner and his abusive behavior was catalyzed by an increase in the severity of abuse:

> The last time he hit me with a board. I realized that this guy could really be dangerous. I actually saw him as totally different than the guy I dated. I saw him as someone mean, someone vicious, and I hated him.

> We got into it pretty heavy. And I was emotionally distraught because after that [medical] checkup and stuff . . . we got into it pretty heavy. And he just turned around and smacked me and knocked me into the bed and I was bleeding real bad. The next day I woke up and my nose was all puffy and I had two black eyes. But he was real sorry after that and I told him to get the hell out, and there was no way I was going to put up with that anymore.

It was almost as though the abuse had been nearly invisible to her, given the push to construct the aggression as not his fault and to take blame on herself for provoking him. As long as the physical aggression remained at a fairly low level, she was able to keep it below the surface as "nonabusive behavior." However, when the aggression reached a point where it began to accelerate in severity, it helped the woman fundamentally reframe what was happening to her as abusive, undeserved, and unacceptable behavior.

Often, reconstructing his abuse as a negative behavior that she did not deserve occurred in the context of a conversation or interaction with friends or family:

> My brother walked in right after it happened, and M was standing over me and I was sitting in a chair and M started to cry and say "I've done something awful." And he wanted my brother to hit him. My brother said he wouldn't hit anyone, and the worst thing to do would be to hit a woman. . . . My brother was the cause when he said no real man would do that. I guess that was the climactic point. I had lost my feelings for M, but then I realized I had a better self-concept for myself. I deserved better than that.

> I went home and I went out with my friend T and I had the best time. It was a whole different world from what I was used to, and that made me start thinking about things. It made me open my eyes and I said, "I'm not putting up with it anymore!"

Thus, interaction with significant others proved to be a powerful force in the reconstruction of his behavior as unacceptable and in the rebuilding of her own sense of self-worth. Furthermore, when the actual time of leaving the abusive partner took place, many of the young women spoke of the importance of the help they received from family and friends:

> [After a severe bout of physical abuse] I barricaded myself in my bedroom. I had a butcher knife from the kitchen and I pushed all the furniture I could against the door. They [her boyfriend and a friend of his] came in at 11 p.m., and tried to get in. I waited until 3 a.m., until they passed out, and I walked out the door. I went to a phone booth and called my mom and told her to come get me. I told her why I was scared to leave. I sat in the telephone booth for 6 hours until my mom got there.

> I went back to my apartment just bawling, and [I ran into a male friend] and he said, "What happened? No, don't tell me what happened to your face. S did it! You just stay away from him." He took me upstairs to my apartment and put some ice on my face and was telling me to stay away from S. The next night, another guy came over because they heard that S was going to come over.

These findings echo the work that Ferraro and Johnson (1983) described in their classic article titled "How Women Experience Battering: The Process of Victimization." The battered women they described also spoke about how an increase in the severity of the abuse, interaction with friends and family, or both, catalyzed a change in the perception of the batterer's abusive behavior and helped them move from an ethic of trying to save the batterer or worrying about taking the children away from their father to the belief that they did not deserve the abuse and should leave. Our study is consistent with previous studies in highlighting the importance of social support in helping an abused woman leave (Barnett & LaViolette, 1993; Barnett, Miller-Perrin, & Perrin, 1997; NiCarthy, 1987).

❧ A Final Note

As a final note to this chapter, we address the question of how the experiences of the young women who had been physically and psychologically abused during courtship are both similar to and different from the experiences of battered women who are married or in longer-term cohabiting relationships. Some of the most obvious differences are related to the fact that women in marital or long-term cohabiting relationships typically are more economically dependent on their abusers. In addition, married or cohabiting women often are in the position of both protecting and worrying about the future of their dependent children. These barriers can serve as significant entanglements that make extrication from the web of abuse a longer and more difficult process (Carlson, 1997; Kirkwood, 1993; Rosen, 1996).

Despite these differences, though, we are struck by the many similarities that we saw between the narratives provided by the young women we interviewed and the narratives provided by battered women who are or were in longer-term relationships. For example, the young women we interviewed clearly identified the myriad ways that control was an important dynamic in the abuse, and their stories of control are very reminiscent of those recounted in classic works on wife battering. The role of jealousy, the fear of abandonment, and the complex interplay of self-blame and excusing the aggressor are also common themes in both our work and studies of wife-battering relationships (e.g., Dobash & Dobash, 1979; Dutton, 1988; Dutton & Golant, 1995; Kirkwood, 1993; NiCarthy, 1987; Stets, 1988; Walker,

1979). Indeed, it is chilling to read a narrative of control and jealousy and suddenly remember that the speaker is an 18-year-old teenager who is describing her high school boyfriend. The roots of male control of relationships and future patriarchal terrorism began very early in the relationships these young women described for us. Tragically, abusive relationships can have the same horrendous consequences of homicide and permanent injury even when the aggressor and victim are still legally considered "children."

Ultimately, the women who shared their stories with us displayed incredible fortitude and agency in the face of destructive behavior at the hands of a loved one. Although the men's abusive behavior did affect the women's sense of self-worth both at the time of the abuse and subsequently, the vast majority of the women we studied nevertheless actively resisted their partners' control and eventually left the abusive situation. Although the abuse had a strong impact on how the women viewed themselves and their relationships with men in the future, every one of the women also talked about the strength of their survivorship.

4

❦

"I Never Called It Rape"

Sexual Aggression
in Dating Relationships

Linda came to the interview to talk about an incident that occurred one night when she was 13 and her girlfriend was 14 years old. Shortly into the interview, she stopped, looked at me with shock and the dawning of understanding in her eyes, and said that she'd just realized she had been sexually coerced in another relationship later in her life. (It was not uncommon for the women to reach the end of the interview and make a hesitant comment to the effect that, "I suppose I should have told you about the relationship [or incident] with J, too!" And we would start at the beginning again.)

When Linda was 13, she and her girlfriend happened to meet two older boys at an arcade. They offered to drive them home and, after disagreeing (Linda said "No," her friend said "Yes"), they went. They ended up parking, where the boys took the girls out of the car and into the woods, separating them. Linda was forced onto the ground and, when she would not have sex with the boy, he straddled her and forced her to perform oral sex. She remembers that she didn't know what was happening and thinking he was going to kill her. Eventually, he was distracted by the presence of other people in the area and took her back to the car. The girls were driven to the girl-friend's house in silence. Afterward, Linda says they held each other and cried and never spoke of that night again.

The next situation she described occurred when she was a fresh-man in high school, dating a senior. They had dated for several months when she realized a pattern was evolving. They would go to parties and he would try to get her to drink and then would force himself on her. She would usually be able to stop him before things went "too far," but she began to resent this behavior and the attitude that he expected sex from her. Eventually, they broke up.

Since then, Linda says that she has had few relationships but would like to find someone to love. Although she had been in ther-apy, Linda always felt that the incident that occurred when she was 13 was her fault because she placed herself in a dangerous situation and should therefore reap the consequences. She finds it difficult to enjoy herself or to let herself be happy, feels she has little worth, and is wary of people. She says she feels "quietly ashamed." She is uncomfortable with sex, even in a relationship that lasted 2 years, especially oral sex. She has never had an orgasm and thinks she never will. At the time of the interview, Linda described herself as a recovering anorexic and felt that she was entering a better phase of her life.

Twenty-three women discussed with us their experiences of sexual aggression in their dating relationships. Their stories provide a collage of haunting and inspiring images. Their relationships, their struggle to understand what happened to them, to cope, and to move on seemed at times like vivid snapshots of moments fro-zen in time and at others like a home movie with the woman herself behind the camera providing narrative asides and editing. An interesting phenomenon occurred during the interview process in that many of the women displayed what at first seemed a curi-ous detachment when describing the actual sexual aggression. Although they were emotional in most cases, it was almost as if they were describing another person. When they discussed other issues, however, their demeanor shifted toward more adamant and closer ownership of the experiences, thoughts, and feelings they expressed. On further consideration and examination of the interviews, it became clear this was a valid observation and that these acts of sexual aggression had indeed happened to another person: a person they used to be, younger and naive and innocent, but that way no longer.

In this chapter, we describe (a) the sexual aggression experiences, (b) the dynamics of the relationship, (c) the dynamics of control, and (d) the ways in which women sought to construct meaning around their experiences of sexual aggression. The interconnectedness of our analysis of relational dynamics, control, and constructing meaning is depicted in Figure 4.1.

❧ The Sexual Aggression Experiences

The types of sexual aggression experienced by these women varied greatly based on many factors. Age and sexual experience arose as important concerns, as did type of relationship and the type and patterns of aggression. For the purposes of our study, we defined sexual aggression as sexual interaction that is gained against one's will through the use of physical force, threat of force, pressure, incapacitation, or use of position of authority (based on Koss, 1988). In this chapter, we use the term *aggression* as the most general term to refer to any behaviors within that definition. We use the term *coercion* to refer to forced sexual contact and acts excluding intercourse, and the term *rape* to refer to intercourse either by physical force or verbal or contextual manipulation (i.e., harassment or the use of alcohol, drugs, etc.).

Age and Level of Sexual Experience

The age range of the respondents at the time of the study was 18 to 38 years, with the average being 24.7 years of age. The mean age at which the women first experienced aggression was 17 years (ranging from 13 to 25 years); their perpetrators were 18 years old (ranging from 16 to 24 years). Initially, each woman came to the interview to describe a specific incident of sexual aggression and the dynamics of her relationship with that perpetrator. However, as the interviews

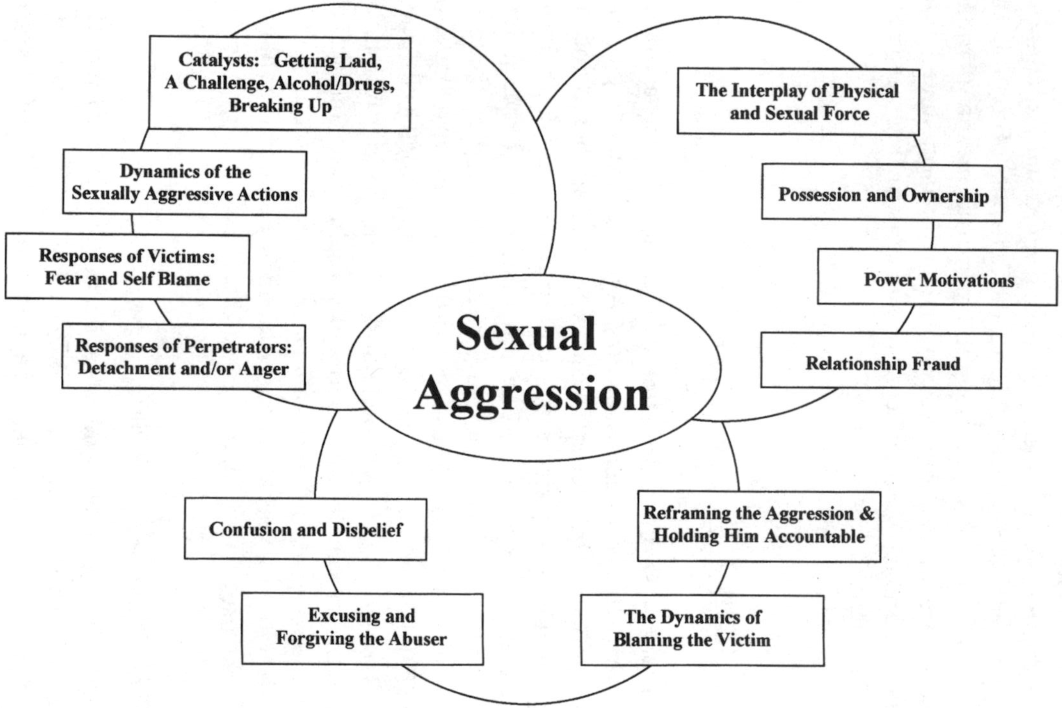

Figure 4.1. Constructing Meaning Around Sexual Aggression

The Interplay of Physical and Sexual Force

Possession and Ownership

Power Motivations

Relationship Fraud

Reframing the Aggression & Holding Him Accountable

The Dynamics of Blaming the Victim

Sexual Aggression

Catalysts: Getting Laid, A Challenge, Alcohol/Drugs, Breaking Up

Dynamics of the Sexually Aggressive Actions

Responses of Victims: Fear and Self Blame

Responses of Perpetrators: Detachment and/or Anger

Confusion and Disbelief

Excusing and Forgiving the Abuser

Table 4.1   Sexual Aggression Experiences

	Number	Percent	Age Occurred Range	Mean	Total Number of Incidents
Rape					
Virgins	5	23.8	14-26	18	5
Nonvirgins	9	42.9	16-24	17	16+
Forced oral sex					
Virgins	3	14.3	13-16	14	3
Nonvirgins	1	4.8	20	20	2
Forced fondling					
Virgins	5	23.8	14-21	18	7
Pressured consensual intercourse[a]					
Virgins	4	19.0	13-18	15	4

NOTE: $N = 21$ (due to missing data from 2 respondents).
a. Respondent indicated that she "gave in" to his pressure to engage in intercourse.

progressed, most of the women also relayed information on other incidents of sexual aggression by other perpetrators. Thus, 74% of the women interviewed (17 out of 23) reported experiencing sexual aggression in more than one relationship; overall, during the interviews the women described between 1 and 9 (an average of 2 to 3) separate sexually aggressive incidents.

Combined with age, the individual's level of sexual experience establishes a fundamental basis for understanding the dynamics of these women's lives, relationships, and expectations (see Table 4.1). For example, 66% of the women reported having experienced rape. Twenty-four percent of the respondents were virgins at the time of the rape, corresponding precisely with the findings of Abma, Driscoll, and Moore (1998). (In our study, if we include those women who as virgins reluctantly "gave in" to the pressure to have sex, this figure rises to 42.8%, which is very close to the 41% figure found by Koss, 1988.) Fourteen percent of the sample were forced to perform oral sex when they were virgins, reporting much fear and little understanding of the act. To summarize, for almost one third of the women in this study, their first experience with sex and sexuality was violent and forced. This is a sobering statistic that had tremendous

implications for the ways in which they viewed romantic relationships and themselves.

Relationship Context

Sexual aggression occurred within the full range of heterosexual
relationship types, including acquaintances, casual dating, serious
dating, engagement and subsequent marriage, living together, and
friendships. A typical relationship in which aggression occurred was,
therefore, difficult to pinpoint. Some women did not define what happened to them as occurring within the context of a romantic relationship. They referred to the perpetrator as a "platonic friend" or to dating a person "a couple times" before the incident. For example, one
woman recounted an incident with a friend:

> One guy was a friend of mine for 3 or 4 years—a friend only. I was
> watching TV with him one night at his house and his parents weren't
> there and he started kissing me. He got on top of me, he tried to take off
> my blouse! All in about 2 minutes. I was trying to stop him gently
> because I didn't want to hurt his feelings, but he just wouldn't quit.
> Finally, I had to get really angry and yell at him.

Other long-term romantic relationships (e.g., this one of 8 years'
duration) became sexually aggressive only at the point of breakup:

> Then right at the end of our relationship, when I was breaking up with
> him, he sat on me one time for 2 hours and wouldn't let me move. He
> just sat there and cried and then we had sex because he made me. . . . I
> just did it so he would get off me and go away and leave me alone.

It is interesting to note that all of the relationships in which sexual
aggression occurred eventually ended. This parallels findings that
appear in the work of Mary Koss (1988), which reported that 87% of
the relationships ended.

The Interplay of Sexual and Physical Aggression

All the women described the use of physical force in their depictions of sexual aggression (i.e., most frequently being physically restrained, held or pinned down, and/or pushed or shoved). Ironically,
though, only 48% reported that they had experienced any type of

physical violence when asked to respond to the violence items on the Conflict Tactics Scale (Straus, 1979). For example, one woman answered in response to the physical violence question:

> No. Not unless you consider that in probably three different relationships the guy would be on top of me or holding me down when I wanted to get up.

Some women dealt more with semantics, calling it physical "force" but not "aggression or violence." For example:

> He was on top of me. He was a pretty strong guy. . . . He was being very physically forceful and he kept saying and trying to convince me.

Another woman took issue with the differentiation between "force," "aggression," and "violence":

> How come you don't call that violence? [in response to a question using the term *sexual aggression*] Because he didn't hit me? I think force can be called violence. I don't see a difference. I think it was physical violence when I stopped struggling and he continued and I was violated. I don't think violence has to appear in the shape of a closed fist . . . or a weapon.

The intriguing aspect of this definitional issue is how people come to accept one term for a particular type of behavior over another term. It is a process that involves the dynamics of the relationship and the ways in which we construct sense out of what happens to us. We speculate that, as articulated by the previous anecdote, many of the women saw physical and sexual aggression as related aspects of the same event:

> I combine the two—physical and sexual aggression. I see it all as sexual aggression in that relationship.

Thus, in the minds of these women, the experiences that they described were traumatic and sexual in nature (that was, after all, the reason they were talking to us). For many, any physical force or violence that was used was done within the primary context of sexual coercion or assault (i.e., as a means for gaining sex). Therefore, it may not have been possible or probable for them to cognitively differentiate between forms of aggression when these behaviors were so enmeshed within the traumatic event itself.

Here, it becomes important to revisit the discursive aspect of relationship violence and, in particular, the definition of violence. It is imperative that we "listen" to the definitions these women have for the violence in their own relationships. Otherwise, we run the risk of missing, silencing, or changing their voices and thereby perpetuating the dominant discourse regarding what exactly constitutes sexual aggression and physical aggression in dating relationships. Although it may seem ironic to us, the "experts," that these women are somehow missing the point or denying that physical abuse occurred in their relationships, we must take a constructivist stance and ask the question, "What makes them define their situations in such a manner?" Failure to do so marginalizes their experience, of which their definitions and interpretations of events are an integral part.

❧ The Relational Dynamics of Sexual Aggression

As with physical aggression, the relational dynamics of sexual aggression are complex. Here, four themes emerged regarding the interactions that occurred in the relationship. These include: catalysts (precipitators) to aggression, the dynamics of the sexually aggressive acts, responses of victims, and responses of perpetrators.

Catalysts to Aggression

Unlike physical abuse, in which the precipitators of violence appear to be unpredictable and varied, the catalysts for sexual aggression in this study seemed fairly clear-cut. The women were able to articulate the reasons for the aggressive episodes quite eloquently. These included "getting laid," a challenge, alcohol or drug use, and breaking up.

"Getting Laid." Primary among the catalysts to sexual aggression was sexual satisfaction. Many women cited the fact that he just wanted "to get laid" as the major reason for his aggression. In fact, 65% of the women ($n = 15$) considered this the most significant catalyst for their experiences. One woman said of several incidents of aggression:

> It's either because you look sexy and they want to have sex with you [or] maybe so they can tell their friends they had sex with you. I don't know what it is. It doesn't seem like they do it to make you happy. Maybe they want to do it, then move on to other relationships.

Frequently in their explanations, women discuss the influence of men's sexual pride. Several saw their assaults as stemming from this issue. For example, some women attributed assaults to "ego":

> I think in all of [the aggressive experiences] it was just their ego. They valued their self-worth and how good a person they were by how well they performed or how many notches they could put on the bed.

> I believe I was raped because he just couldn't take the frustration of me having sex with his friend but not having sex with him. I think it was his ego. I think he was having sex for his ego, not for the gratification.

Another woman revealed a sense of humor when she described one aggressive experience:

> With G, that was the guy I'd been friends with a long time . . . I think his self-esteem was in his penis. He measured his self-worth by what he could do sexually. Outside of that, he didn't think he had any other talents.

A Challenge. Many women felt targeted for aggression because they were a challenge. They were virgins or did not fool around. Therefore, scoring with them added another trophy to the man's collection. One woman looked back on the relationship in which she was forced to have sex and lost her virginity:

> I was a virgin until I was almost 18. . . . He had been pressuring me since day one. . . . He told me I was a challenge. . . . I was a pretty popular person . . . in that I didn't sleep around with guys and my friends did. He went out with me for that simple reason and he got what he wanted, regardless of what I felt about it.

This woman talks about the person who date raped her:

He was very weird. He wanted to be the first person to have sex with me. He was obsessed with taking girls' virginity away. He had talked to me about girls he dated before me. For example, my girlfriend's boy-friend got to her before he did. That was a lot of what motivated him . . . his own gratification.

Alcohol and/or Drug Use. As we examined the interviews, it became obvious in many cases that the women identified several factors as concurrent catalysts for their experiences. For example, it was re-ported that 57% of the people involved in 19 incidents of aggression were using alcohol and/or drugs. Of that figure, 54% of the perpetra-tors were drinking and/or high. In 46% of the sample, both were drinking and/or high.

Many of the women described what led up to the aggression as being party situations. This woman explained her rape by a "buddy" who frequented the bar in which she worked:

He came in very drunk. . . . He started off in the beginning of the night [in the bar] saying he wanted to make love to me and I guess he just got it in his mind he wanted to do that and took it upon himself to force me or force the situation. . . . He started by voicing his opinion and then he ended by physically doing it. What made him use force and verbal coer-cion was the alcohol. I had never seen him that drunk.

One woman's answer in response to a question about a pattern of coercion was the following:

A lot of times we would go out and party and drink and this would hap-pen at night afterwards. Alcohol would make him sexually active and he would just get mad at me because I wouldn't give in.

This woman was philosophical about the role of alcohol in sexual aggression. She contemplated what made her boyfriend violently rape her:

B was drunk. When a man's drunk, he seems to think that just because he wants it, everybody else wants it too. It's like that one little piece of anatomy controls everything they do. Especially if they are drunk.

Even when the respondent reported that both had been drinking, her own use of alcohol was not described in terms of a causal factor for the aggression. From her perspective, however, the perpetrator's drinking did trigger the aggression. Almost without exception, the women talk about being "encouraged" to drink. This woman was 14 and had dated an 18-year-old for a short while:

> He was all the time giving me liquor. We was all the time drinking. . . . He started giving me barbiturates. . . . Anyway, I ended up passing out one night and we had intercourse in his truck. . . . I didn't want to but I just woke up at the end of it. That was kind of rape.

Another woman described a casual dating relationship:

> On our sixth or seventh date, he took me to every club in town and I got so drunk that I fell down some stairs and I don't even remember it. . . . Somehow he got me to go [upstairs]. I never had sexual intercourse with him although I did give him oral sex. . . . I think I did it so he would leave me alone. I regret that incident more than anything ever in my life because I satisfied him just to get him to shut up.

Breaking Up. For some women, the sexual aggression they encountered from their boyfriends occurred at the end of their relationship. There may or may not have been coercion throughout the relationship, but there was no doubt as to what was happening when they were trying to end the relationship. As one woman recounted,

> The sexual aggression didn't start until after I broke up with him. We ended up going to Florida together and while [we were] there he pressured me into it by arguments. . . . He would say stuff like, "Let this be a good-bye present." . . . "After this trip, that's it and I'll leave you alone and I'll never talk to you again." Finally, I got sick of it and gave in to him, basically. . . . Then after we got back from Florida, he was like thinking that we could get back together.

This woman talks about breaking up with a man with whom she had had a relationship of 8 years. She just had nose surgery and was driving to work in a snowstorm when he stepped in front of her car, got in when she stopped, and essentially kidnaped her:

> I was just very scared. I was never scared of him before . . . [but due to the nose surgery and trying to break up] I was seeing another part of him that I had never seen before. . . . We drove around for an hour or 2. Finally, I realized I was going to have to have sex with him before he

was going to let me go. . . . We went and rented a hotel room and had sex. I remember being repulsed and I'm sure he probably thought it was like he always did. But I thought it was horrible. . . . I think he thought that if I would have sex with him, I was still his.

Implicit in these examples is the idea that the act of sex indicates possession, the retention of the relationship, and perhaps even caring. In other words, if she would have sex with him, then the relationship was not over. This use of coercion as a tactic of control at the point of breakup was effective in the short term (i.e., they had sex) but was ineffectual in the long term, in that it only postponed the inevitable.

In addition, the discourse of romance (as discussed in Chapter 2) seems to banish power issues through a "myth of equality" and through romance. Yet, also at work is the discursive aspect of gendered perspectives on relationships, one in which maintenance chores are attributed to women and autonomous motives to men. In other words, men and women are empowered differently by romance and, therefore, are given contrasting positions and identities (Wetherell, 1995). When the woman in the relationship seeks to break up, the dominant discourse is challenged because she is no longer passive or reactive, nor is she behaving in stereotypic nurturant, maintenance-oriented ways. Aggression becomes one response strategy for the man in his attempt to restore the balance of the dominant discourse of courtship.

Furthermore, in these aggressive situations, the discourse of romance is at work but within a dysfunctional context, that is, the men may be acting in accordance with the dominant discourse when they commit rape at the point of breakup as an attempt to "initiate" or prove their love. This attempt will make the woman see how much they care and she will love them again. The physical act of intercourse is, therefore, a token of love—proof that they care and that the relationship will remain intact.

The Dynamics of the Sexually Aggressive Actions

In our examination of the aggression found in these relationships, it was evident that the type and dynamics of aggression varied a great deal. A continuum existed that ranged from the least severe sexual coercion (being forced to participate in acts with which the respondent was uncomfortable) to the most severe rape (forced penetration or sexual intercourse). This continuum was very similar to that identified by Christopher (1988).

One woman described a relatively "minor" incident of aggression in which she was coerced physically into acts with which she was uncomfortable:

> There was a movie on so we decided to watch that. We were just watching TV and kissing, [it] wasn't anything really. He started pushing for a few things [and] I was giving into it a little bit. Until he was pressuring me for things I wasn't ready for. There had been a whole lot of fondling. He was trying to get my clothes off and trying for sexual intercourse. I said, "No." He kept pushing and pushing. It reached the point where I had to finally throw him off of me to get the point across. . . . The more I said "no," it was . . . like he was coming on more and more.

Eight of the respondents (35%) described a total of 12 incidents of sexual coercion and alluded to several more. Although coercion may not be considered by many to be as serious an offense as rape, it had a lasting effect on these women's perceptions of both themselves and their relationships with men.

Another woman described a more serious experience when she was 14 in which she was left alone in a car with a boy:

> I did not want to be by myself with him. . . . . He starts kissing me and everything. Next thing I know he's got my hand down his pants. I just kept pulling it back. I think that's obvious enough. If I don't want my hand down there, I do not want my hand there. He kept on and kept on, and finally he whipped that thing out, got a hold of me, and wanted me to give him a blow job. I said "No, I am not going to do that." He just grabs me and shoves my head down there and makes me. I tried to get up but he would not let me up. He kept on and when he came, he still would not let me up. He made me swallow it.

All of the women who described similar experiences indicated the sexual aspect of their subsequent relationships was seriously affected in that they found it extremely unpleasant or impossible to perform oral sex with their partners.

A further example on the continuum is this experience that occurred when this woman was 14 years old:

> He had pulled my blouse off and I had struggled with him and asked him to stop, but he wouldn't stop. I remember that he was older than I was. . . . He was much bigger than I was and stronger. . . . I remember getting so scared that by the time he had his hand in my pants I had just stopped struggling with him and started crying. He put his fingers inside me and I continued to cry and he stopped finally and said, "See? That wasn't so bad!"

Finally, this woman described the loss of her virginity to her boyfriend of 2 months when she was 16 years old:

> He wouldn't let me up off the couch and I was like "Let me up. I have to get ready [to go to a football game]. Mom is going to ask why we weren't there on time." Finally, he said, "You are not getting up this time." He told me he was tired of it . . . and I wasn't getting out of it this time. . . . He took me back to my room. . . . He threw me down on the bed. I thought he was playing so I was laughing it off. He wasn't playing. He proceeded to take all my clothes off me, and then [at that time] I didn't call it rape. . . . It was so bland, a horrible experience.

Often, women's refusals of the sexual overture were perceived as token resistance to be overcome, as one woman noted:

> It seems like with most men if I create any sort of boundary, it is something to be challenged. . . . Like the whole flirting game—that maybe I'm just saying no to stimulate a little conflict which would make things even hotter. . . . It seems as though they are thinking, "Yes, she says she doesn't want to do this, but she really seems to like it."

All of these anecdotes aptly illustrate the dynamics of the traditional sexual script (Byers, 1996; Hare-Mustin, 1994; Kahn, Mathie, & Torgler, 1994; Metts & Spitzberg, 1996). Clearly, as relayed by the young women we interviewed, the men who behaved aggressively toward them had an expectation that they could push for sex, even to the point of coercive and physically forceful behavior. Just as clearly, her attempt to communicate that she was not willing or interested in sexual interaction was viewed as a "token no" by the men. Essentially, her protestations were ignored (Byers, 1996; Byers, Giles, & Price, 1987; Muehlenhard & Hollabaugh, 1988).

These narratives also illustrate the dual role of male privilege and the lack of empathy for the other that is a part of the male sexual script. Not only was it his right to have sex with her (particularly if there was an ongoing relationship between the two), it was also his right to ignore her pleas to stop and her tears. Yet, some of the men may have had an inkling of the impact of their sexual coercion and rape behavior, in that they sought her reassurance that the experience had been "OK."

Responses of Victims

The responses of the women to the aggressive events fall into two categories that can be differentiated primarily by the passage of time. Immediate responses to the sexual aggression included strong physical and emotional reactions, such as crying, physical distancing, fear, and disbelief. The delayed reactions of self-blame and shame, confusion, and resignation to their fate (i.e., the loss of their virginity) quickly followed in a matter of minutes or hours.

The immediate responses of the women were driven by strong emotions. Many times, they reported fear and shock almost simultaneously. This woman described her reaction after a friend had forced her to perform oral sex:

> I was scared to death. I didn't know what to do. I had told him no. He was very strong. I was only 14. It was totally dead outside, it was close to 1:00 in the morning. . . . About that time, their friends showed up. . . . I went home and just cried. I was scared to death to think what would have happened if those guys had not come when they did.

The women talked about getting as far away from the perpetrator afterward as possible, whether in the car, room, or leaving his presence altogether. Another woman described the aftermath of a coercive situation:

> I reacted by basically pushing him off me onto the floor and told him to leave. . . . I was very upset. I was more mad than anything because I felt

like I had been violated because that's not what I wanted. To me that
scared me a lot.

Many women talked about being shocked or totally surprised by
the aggression, such as this woman, who was forced to perform oral
sex:

> I was surprised when *T* did it. That was the first time I have been con-
> fronted with sex. I knew that he might want to kiss me or fondle me, but
> I did not think that he wanted to go all the way. Back then I was a virgin
> so I was not going to do anything.

The surprise is evident in the words of this woman, who was friends
with the man who raped her:

> I had no idea [that this would happen]. *R* [the rapist] knew that I had no
> intention of ever starting anything with him. I was perfectly happy
> with *G*. So I had no idea that anything like [the rape] would happen.

This woman describes her intense feelings during and immediately after the aggression in terms that were heard frequently from
other women in the study:

> We were kissing and things started to happen and before I realized
> what was going on he had penetrated me. We were having sex! And I
> was like, "Wait! This is not supposed to be happening!" And at this
> point I started crying and I pushed him off me. He finished on his own.
> He masturbated and finished his orgasm by himself. The whole time I
> was crying hysterically, just completely devastated that the whole
> thing had happened.

After the initial response to the aggression passed, women experienced a second wave of emotions and reactions. They were no less intense, mingling with initial reactions. For example, the woman just
quoted expressed the feelings of self-blame that were echoed by many
of our respondents:

> I took all the blame on myself [because] he said nothing happened. I
> continued to cry."

Another woman described her fear and self-blame in juxtaposition:

> I remember thinking I would be found dead in the woods the next morning and wondered what my parents would think. . . . I blamed myself. . . . I internalized it as my fault because I went with him. Therefore, I suffered the consequences.

Clearly, an immediate sense of self-blame characterized the reactions of some of the women. As can be seen later in this chapter, the dynamics of self-blame were pervasive for most women for many years after the aggressive experience.

Many women reported that they were embarrassed that they had "allowed themselves to become involved" in a sexually aggressive situation. Embarrassment existed for several reasons and went hand in hand with confusion. Hindsight eventually allowed the participants to identify the source of their confusion as sexual naïveté, inexperience, or misconceptions about the intentions of their partner or the status of the relationship.

This woman talked about her perceptions of the events following her experience with sexual coercion from an older man on a school outing:

> All the way back home I could hardly face any of my friends. I felt like my roommate friend was mad because I hadn't had sex with K and that my other friend was disgusted because she thought I did! Then there were the guys. They all thought I was a tease. Maybe I was. I don't know. But I never meant to be, I just didn't know what this sex thing was all about! I worried about my reputation for a long time after that—a year anyway.

Some women were pragmatic about the course of events. They tried to resign themselves to the fact that they had lost their virginity and that it was time to get on with their lives, as this woman said of her experience:

> I just let it go [the date rape] and I thought it would be the last [time]. But no, he intended to from then on [have a sexual relationship]. Finally, I just gave in. I was real uptight about it. I [said], "J, it's time to just enjoy it and go on. This is the way it's supposed to be.

It is a strikingly prevalent theme that these women accept as the norm unfulfilling sex, discomfort, and disrespect in a sexually intimate relationship. This attitude had incredible implications for their sense of well-being and their expectations for future romantic relationships and partners.

Responses of Perpetrators

If the responses of the victims were pragmatic, those of the perpetrators were even more so. Their behaviors ranged from the unemotional and detached, to the satisfied, to the volatile. Some men behaved as if nothing important had occurred or that the aggression was her fault. This woman recounts her boyfriend's behavior after he had raped her in her own bedroom:

> He was just happy, smiling and going on. And then he acted like it had never happened. He just got up, went to the shower, and I don't know. It was really bad."

This is another such account from the woman who described how her friend forced her to have sex:

> He finishes, he rolls over—I am still crying—[and] he took my face in his hands and said "Stop crying. There's nothing wrong. Nothing happened." I was like "What the hell are you talking about? Of course something happened!" . . . He said "Nothing happened, there's no reason to be bawling. Just quit your crying." . . . He just got up, went upstairs and went to bed. That was it.

Koss (1988) discussed men's perspectives of their involvement in sexual aggression in terms similar to ours. They tended to minimally report negative emotions (i.e., fear, anger, depression) and were more likely to be proud. They felt mildly responsible for the aggression, placing equal or more blame on the woman. Steward (1995) wrote an eloquent, remorseful account of his feelings regarding sex and his rape of a young girl in which he described his behavior as predatory, although he purported to respect women as equals. His use of alcohol to increase her vulnerability and subsequent disregard for her well-being during and after sex are echoed in the stories of the women in this study.

Some women reported that the men were uncaring or detached after the aggression, ignoring them and focusing on their own pleasure. This woman describes her experience throughout the night that her boyfriend physically forced her to have intercourse:

> Now we had done it . . . [it was] irrevocable. It was really crossing the line that was the big issue for me, not whether we did it again or not. . . . I was trying to enjoy it at this point. . . . He was just getting off like a rabbit. It was like it seemed totally for his pleasure and that bothered me. . . . He wasn't trying to give me any pleasure.

In some instances, the men became volatile or angry when the women resisted their sexual advances. Sometimes, their actions included verbal abuse and harassment. This woman recounts her experience over a 4-month period with an older boy:

> He was very forceful, very physically forceful. He would basically try to undress me. . . . He would get really mad and get out of the car and scream and then he would get back in the car and tell me he was never going out with me again. He would call me a bitch and a tease. . . . I had fought him off this one night for a long time. I never said "No," I just held onto my clothes. He put me out of the car and made me walk back up to the road. To this day, I cannot stand to be in the woods by myself.

Another woman experienced severe verbal abuse when she would refuse sex with a man she had dated previously:

> Yeah, [he talked about it] more in terms of "You inconsiderate, unappreciative little bitch. We've been friends for so long, how can you do this to me?" . . . While he was upset, I still felt it was the right thing to do at the time [not have sex]. . . . I haven't seen him since then.

It seems that the women experienced such abuse as a common reaction from the men when they successfully resisted sexual involvement and intercourse. When the behavior was coercive and stopped short of rape, the men exhibited anger, or at least that is the interpretation of the women. It may be logical to assume that there was also frustration vented in these instances. For example, here her friend's angry reaction to her resistance clearly has a woman confused:

> He was so angry at me that that's what I remember to this day. And I
> don't understand—never understood—his indignant attitude! I mean,
> we had been friends for years and I'd never encouraged him. . . . I
> remember him asking why I'd come over to his house in the first place.
> . . . He was livid!

These findings are quite reminiscent of the work that demonstrates that physically abusive men have difficulty identifying their emotions (Dutton, 1988). The masculine stereotype does not provide a model for the appropriate expression of feelings such as frustration, vulnerability, or dependency. Anger, however, is an "appropriate" emotion for men, so men may display anger when being flooded by other feelings (Dutton & Golant, 1995; Levant, 1995a, 1995b).

These findings again reflect the powerful role of the traditional male sexual script and the discourse of sexuality in shaping both men's reactions and the women's reactions to men's sexual aggression. His right to engage in sex no matter what the impact on his partner is chillingly portrayed in these women's narratives. In addition, the separation of feeling from sexuality is all too apparent (for more explication of this script, see Byers, 1996; Carter, 1995; Metts & Spitzberg, 1996).

❧ The Dynamics of Control

Wendy Stock (1991) stated that "rape and other forms of sexual coercion can be viewed as both the expression and confirmation of male power, dominance, and control of women" (p. 62). Many women talked about their partners trying to control them by the use of force. Seventeen of the women (74%) labeled the aggression they experienced as, at least in part, the perpetrator's attempt to control them.

Our analysis of the dynamics of control is somewhat arbitrarily broken down into four sections: control and the interplay of physical and sexual force, possession and ownership, power motivations, and relationship fraud. We call this division arbitrary because the dynamics of control were difficult to portray without seeming to take them out of context; the narratives regarding control were threaded throughout the interview, not just in one section or discussion. In addition, the issue of control already has been alluded to in many other concepts, such as the catalysts of breaking up, getting laid, and a challenge. In reality, upon closer examination, control and the use of sexual and physical forms of aggression are practically inseparable. This created a difficult organizational decision regarding the treatment of the findings.

Control and the Interplay of Physical and Sexual Force

As mentioned earlier in this chapter, the women we interviewed often talked of physical force as an integral component of the sexual aggression they experienced. They did not make fine-tuned differentiations between the two and instead emphasized that his attempts to control or influence her behavior often incorporated physical violence. Thus, we saw a strong connection between the use of physical force and sexual aggression as forms of control.

For some, the issue of physical control arose when the woman did not want to have sexual relations:

> The only thing that would make him violent is when I would tell him that I didn't want to have sex. That was it. . . . I would give in. . . . There was only one time that I didn't give in because he would hurt me. I mean he wouldn't like punch me to hurt me, but he would like hold me down and pry my legs apart. That would hurt me and that would be why I would give in.

In instances such as this, it may be that the women do not distinguish between the physical and sexual aggression because of the overriding factor of control. In other words, the end result, her capitulation, obscures the means to such an extent that the adjectives "physical" and "sexual" are redundant and meaningless.

Others reported that their partners' use of physical force was a strategy used to gain immediate control of and compliance from the women. Some women indicated that the use of physical force made the perpetrator feel "more like a man," more masculine. Ultimately, the issues of domination raised in Chapter 3 were reflected in the interviews with the women who had experienced sexual aggression. This narrative is from a woman who reported that her boyfriend regularly abused her both physically and sexually:

I think he was trying to beat me into submission. He wanted me to be a real passive person. Just to sit and listen to anything he said and not say anything.

At times, sexual coercion played a role after the physical abuse. One woman describes the abusive behavior of her husband that occurred both before and after their marriage:

After we would get in a fight, he would hit me. He would think if he could get me in the bed and have sex with me, I would forget about him hitting me. He had proven he loved me even though he had just hit me and that would justify him hitting me. He's really screwed up, I think, but every time he would beat me up he'd want to make love to me afterwards. . . . I think he thought he could get back into my good graces.

Another example involves feelings of having been taken advantage of as well:

My "ex" used to sexually take advantage of me. Every time he got physically violent with me, he would force me to have sex with him because he wanted to make it up to me. He was a con artist . . . a good salesman.

This idea of "making everything all right" with sex is a particularly insidious form of sexual coercion. It was the element of establishing and maintaining control that was justification for his behavior if, for example, the woman refused sex after a beating and was subsequently raped. He had gotten his way and now sex was proof that he cared. For some, sex was almost an apology for the physical abuse.

The men were not always the only ones to use physical aggression. Six women (26%) reported hitting the men who abused them as well. In all cases, it was clearly motivated by revenge, as indicated by one woman:

I was trying to hurt him. . . . When the odds were in my favor of winning, that's when I would hit him . . . when he was drunk or passed out. . . . That way he never knew I hit him. . . . I threw a chair at him. . . . I glued his penis with Crazy Glue one time. It didn't hold. He didn't have to go to the hospital. I tried!

Another woman recounted her use of violence after her live-in boyfriend would pass out after abusing her both physically and sexually. One time she hit him with his boot, giving him a black eye and a lump on the head, which he later thought he'd gotten while drinking. She said it made her feel good that she'd hurt him, too.

None of these women reported using violence in circumstances other than this (i.e., while he was incapacitated). It is interesting to note that, although many women did struggle with the perpetrator, they did not consider themselves to have used physical violence. Their pushing, shoving, and kicking was all part of their defense against the sexual aggression that was directed toward them. As with the physical aggression chapter and other research, it is clear here that men and women hit for different reasons (Emery & Lloyd, 1994). In the case of this study, it seems that men hit *to* control, whereas women hit when they *could* control (i.e., to retaliate).

Possession and Ownership

Possession and ownership also were reflected in the narratives of the women who had experienced sexual aggression. Many of the interviewees talked about the ways in which sexual interaction implied that he now owned her. At times, the fact that they had a dating relationship seemed to contribute to his feelings of ownership:

> I think that since we dated for a while, he thought that I had become his, you know, his property and that he had the right to at least try to have sex with me. And I think that he truly believed that if we dated, you know, if he took me out, paid for movies, pizzas, spent time with me, that he should have sex with me! So I guess it was that he was trying to establish his possession of me, to have control over me. When I think back on it, it was a real power play on his part.

Another woman described the possessive motivation for her boyfriend's physical and sexual aggression in this way:

> I think he was just trying to keep me. I don't think he loved me. He was very obsessed with me. It got to the point where my parents had to put a restraining order out on him so the police could keep him away from me.

In another extremely violent example of obsession, a woman described her experience with a boyfriend after she moved out of their house and was asking for time to consider his marriage proposal:

> It was like his face iced over. It wasn't the same person that I was looking at. . . . His voice even changed and he said, "You just fucked up because you aren't going to leave my house alive." At that point he tried to kill me for 4½ hours. . . . I had teeth marks all over my face, hands, and arms. He tried to throw me down the stairs. He tried to put a butcher knife through my head and I ducked. He took me up to the bedroom at knife-point. He had a knife to my back and he said, "Don't do anything stupid. I'm going to make love to you and show you how much I love you." I said, "I don't want you to make love to me, M." He said, "Oh, yes you do." I tried to get up once and forgot where the door was. I had tried to get my clothes first and that's where I messed up. He heard me. . . . He forced me back in the bed and he raped me again, normally and orally, too. He bit me, too—all over the place. I let him snore a good half an hour before I moved again.

She then explained that she thought her attempt to ease out of the possessive relationship made him "insanely" desperate to keep her in it at all costs. (This excerpt also makes our point about context. It would be just as easy and accurate to use this as an example in the section on "breakups," given the content of the quote. However, within the interview it was clear that she was talking about an extreme attempt at control, which made its inclusion more appropriate at this juncture.)

This anecdote is also an example of the connection between the use of physical and sexual aggression as a tactic of control and the discourse of romance. Here, sexual violence is portrayed by the perpetrator as a sign of his love for the woman (albeit a warped sign to all but the perpetrator). We speculate that our cultural discourse for romance and sexuality "in extremis" leads to such desperate distortions of sexuality and hurtful expressions of love.

Power Motivations

The women we interviewed talked about sexual aggression in terms of the perpetrators gaining power over them, on both psychological and emotional levels, in addition to the obvious attempt to influence their behavior (have oral sex, intercourse, etc.). Some women reported few nuances in this power motivation, commenting only on the perpetrator's desire for power. As one woman said of the three separate, serious incidents of aggression:

> [It gave them] a feeling of power, a feeling of control. Feeling they had power over me.

One woman had been violated several years earlier by an older boy. She was asked what she believed he had hoped to accomplish:

> Logically, I'll say power. From a gut level, I'm not sure.

A level of uncertainty is not uncommon in replies even after several years had passed since the incident. The influence of education plus the healing distance that time provided allowed for introspection and some answers to the question "Why?" As these women have shown, however, their own justification for such harmful behavior was elusive, and the answers could still be simplistic when the aggression was a singular event.

In other cases, the coercion and aggression were long-term, occurring within a continuing relationship. Women describing this type of experience were more articulate in their understanding of the men's motivations. They discussed a variety of scenarios. For example, this woman said she never willingly consented to have sex with her boyfriend and talked about his control and the sexual coercion:

> He would maybe ask me if it was as bad as I thought it would be or [he'd ask] well why did I say "No"? He had a nice time . . . and I would say, "Well, I don't like it. I don't like it." He would always try and make me change my mind. . . . I think that he was thinking that he would lose some control over me and I guess he wanted to make me learn to like [sex] and him in that way.

Changing her mind about sex in this instance was a sign of his power over her. In another example, power over sex was merely one of the many attempts at control that pervaded the whole relationship with this man:

> I suppose he thought if I wouldn't consent to [sex] that he really had no control over me and he really had all these little strict rules for me. . . . I

just kind of scoffed at [them] and laughed because they were silly little things that didn't make sense. Well, like "You can't go out drinking with your friends unless I'm with you." . . . I couldn't wear a skirt out with my friends. . . . There would always be the comments like "nice slut skirt" and he would always call me names like "slut" or "whore" when he knew that I wasn't.

Relationship Fraud

Another category with which to explain the dynamics of sexual aggression as control involves the use of deceit and manipulation or "relationship fraud." Some of the perpetrators' attempts to control sexual interaction were quite subtle, involving promises that he really did care for her and want to be involved in a committed relationship. This form of coercion was devastating when the woman realized that his real motivation was sex and sex alone. Frequently, women described these perpetrators as sweet-talkers, manipulative, self-centered, and con artists. Forty-eight percent of the respondents talked about having been manipulated into having sex against their will through relationship fraud.

For example, this woman said she could tell when he would try to force her to have sex:

> He became manipulative. [He] would start complimenting me, get close to me . . . get in touch with me. But it didn't feel real. [He] had an ulterior motive.

Another woman describes one of her dating experiences with a boyfriend who knew she had been sexually coerced several times in a previous relationship:

> He took me out, treated me good, never pressed me for anything. . . . I told him I knew what he was doing. . . . I said, "Spending money is not the way to my heart. . . . I just want to be happy." We dated for 2 months. He said, "I really care for you, J." He didn't talk me into it, but he made me think that he cared deeper than he did and he managed to have his way with me. . . . He knew that I had higher values than to just be some drunken slob and just jump in the sack with him. . . . You know, I consented. I'm not trying to excuse that fact. I'm just saying that I cared about him and I thought I was falling in love with him.

This woman describes her feelings after her date finally stopped just short of rape. The interviewer asked what happened next:

> Well, that was the part that affects me as much as the sexual stuff. He just rolls over and goes to sleep. I wanted to talk about why I didn't want to do it. I wanted him to realize that it wasn't anything that was his fault, but that I wasn't ready to have sex with anyone yet. You see, I was still under the misconception that he wanted more than just sex. That lasted about another 5 minutes, because I couldn't talk to him. He just ignored me and went to sleep. . . . I was crushed.

One woman experienced her boyfriend's coercion over a period of time that culminated in date rape. She equated this coercion to a movie character, a "womanizer," who always told the women what they wanted to hear to have sex with them:

> That's kind of what happened with B. [He] would keep progressing a little bit further. . . . Once he said, "You can trust me. We will just lie here." Then it went beyond that and he was forceful about that. . . . Then it kept becoming more [at other times]. . . . I told him why I was scared [to have sex]. I gave him some solid emotional, logical, and health reasons why this made no sense to me. It was something I couldn't do.

Finally, this woman describes her boyfriend's continued coerciveness after date rape occurred in their relationship:

> And if he wanted to have sex then he had sex and I laid there and it was over. . . . He is just very manipulative and he knows what you want to hear. He would say enough to keep me wanting to see him, to think maybe there's hope. Maybe he does care something for me [other] than just wanting to have sex and he knew what I wanted to hear.

In contrast to the previous examples of coercion and aggression in long-term relationships, 6 of the respondents (26%) described date rape as the beginning of the sexual aspect of their relationship with the offender. One woman described the aftermath of date rape:

> From that point on it just got easier to do it, to have sex with him than to fight him off. He got violent. He was mean. He would hold me down and force me to have sex with him almost every time. I wouldn't have done it if he hadn't forced me.

Another woman commented,

> I never ever wanted willingly to consent, ever. He never gave me the chance, so whenever it came up, well, my immediate reaction was "Well, no." It was just pain. I just thought it was something bad.

Thus, there was no one reason why the women continued the relationship and the sex when it was not something that they wanted. They themselves seemed to say that they were naive about sex and relationships or thought that this was the way it was supposed to be. Some women actually had feelings for the offender. It is safe to say, however, that control does continue to play a role, albeit a covert one, particularly at the emotional level. This woman talks about just that:

> I feel really violated, that he just used me for . . . whatever he wanted. Especially since I have feelings for him. I know it would have been different if it was somebody I didn't know who just flat-out raped me.

Logic tells us that this scenario is very common in dating relationships. Unfortunately, we suspect that many women may view this pattern of relationship fraud and sexual manipulation as the norm. What becomes clear is that emotions strongly color the event. Whether the women experienced coercion or aggression at the beginning, throughout, or at the end of a relationship, a common theme among these women was their fervent desire to understand the multilayered emotions surrounding the event, both their own and the perpetrator's. The pressure to prove one's love through sex seemed even more confusing to these women than the instances of physical abuse.

These women's discussions of how sexual coercion played out within the context of an ongoing dating relationship shed light on previous findings by Mary Koss (1988). She reported that 42% of the victims of date rape do have sex with the offender again. Critics of that research question the validity of the finding (e.g., Gilbert, 1993), the implication being that if an unmarried woman has sex with a man after he has raped her, then it must have been consensual in the first place. This line of reasoning has sparked a controversy that has spilled over into popular print. Feminists and women's advocates and their critics have spent much energy in debating the accuracy of the reported prevalence and very existence of date rape as well as how to deal with it (Gilbert, 1993; Koss & Cook, 1993; Paglia, 1995; Pollitt, 1995; Roiphe, 1995).

The diverse experiences of the women in our study do not support the simplistically narrow logic of the critics but instead demonstrate that women continue to have sex with the perpetrator of the date rape for a variety of reasons. In Koss's (1988) study, it was not clear whether the women were forced or willing in the subsequent sexual encounters. In our study, the issue of consent is shown to be misleading, as the data reveal that there are several levels of force and willingness at work in sexually aggressive episodes. We agree with Shotland (1989, 1992), who contended that women's responses to date rape depend on the length and seriousness of the relationship (i.e., longer, serious relationships will likely continue after the aggression compared with short-term, casual relationships). The concern is contextual rather than consensual.

Summary of the Dynamics of Control

As in the chapter on physical aggression, what we describe here is a multifaceted view of the dynamics of control and sexual aggression. For some of the women, sexual aggression, physical aggression, and control were so intertwined as to be inextricable in their narratives. For others, power motivations seemed to describe the underlying dynamics best. Still others emphasized the role of possession and of relationship fraud.

What are the underlying dimensions of all of these examples of control? Once again, we emphasize the discourse of romance and male privilege in relationships in juxtaposition with the traditional sexual script. For women, romance emphasizes the importance of sexual interaction in the context of a close and caring relationship, and the female sexual script emphasizes her role as the "brakes" in their sexual interaction. This sets the stage for potential relationship fraud and coercive manipulation and for blaming the woman should sexual interaction go too far. Male privilege and the traditional male sexual script, on the other hand, set the stage for his use of any means to gain sexual interaction and his sense of rightful ownership of the woman with whom he is involved. It is no wonder that romantic relationships are so confusing and negotiating sexual interaction so difficult. Still, it is frightening how very often these perceived cultural imperatives of male sexuality spill into aggressive behavior. It is almost as if the message "sex no matter what the cost to the woman" has been socialized right into the fabric of the male sexual script.

Finally, we speculate on how control through physical force and control through sexual force are different. In reading the women's narratives, our sense was that the men's use of physical aggression played into the immediacy of control and influence over the woman, her behavior, and person. Sexual aggression, in contrast, represented a more pervasive phenomenon, in that it defined the very relationship between the man and the woman. The women talked about the sexual abuse as not only controlling them individually but also as controlling the dynamics and course of the relationship as well as the ways in which they thought about relationships thereafter. As such, sexual aggression was more upsetting to these women than was the physical aggression, causing much distress, recrimination, and mistrust. Sexual aggression served to emphasize for these women that they were vulnerable and open not only to attack but also to manipulation from relative strangers and loved ones alike.

❧ "Constructing Meaning" Around the Experience of Sexual Aggression

Like our research on physical aggression, a major focus of this study centers on the ways in which these women came to make some sense out of what happened to them. As in Chapter 3, we discuss interrelated phases of this construction process. These themes deal with confusion, excusing and forgiving the aggressor, the dynamics of blaming the victim, and, finally, how holding the aggressor accountable allowed the women to reframe the event and move on in their lives and relationships.

Confusion

In the sexual aggression study, women had difficulty acknowledging that what they had experienced was aggression. Many never had a name or label for what happened to them or considered the coercion or forced intercourse to be anything other than a normal part of dating relationships. As Robin Warshaw (1988) found in her book *I Never Called It Rape*, many of these women denied the reality of their experience. This woman's response was typical:

> While I was talking to him about [the fact that she did not want to have sex], he was getting on top of me. . . . I felt that, hopefully, he was hearing me and he said something like, "You mean you don't want to?" I was trying to be real tactful and diplomatic and all this stuff. I said, "Of course, I want to, but . . ." and boom! He was inside. I never really thought of it as date rape until very recently. I just always thought of it as my fault that I let things get out of hand.

This quotation also clearly represents the link between these women's reactions to and definitions of what happened to them. In other words, if a woman takes responsibility for the aggression (which we have seen that many women did) then it becomes difficult, if not impossible, to call it "rape." This explains, in part, the internal dissonance that these women experienced in their attempts to construct meaning from the emotional and psychological aftermath of the event.

We turn to the discourse of courtship for messages that reinforce this assumption. Relevant to our reasoning is that part of the traditional sexual script that says that women must resist a man's sexual overtures and at the same time ensure that he still remain interested romantically (Byers, 1996). This set of expectations for women greatly influences the dynamics of sexual coercion. As in the previous example, self-blame is almost ensured in such a scenario where the woman is trying to be "tactful and diplomatic" in her refusal. Given this, the women are incredibly yet understandably myopic in their assessment of the event. The terms *rape* and *coercion*, therefore, exist outside their realm of understanding and personal experience.

Byers et al. (1987) found that women tended to refuse sexual overtures less definitely or assertively if they occurred within a romantic relationship. This concept is supported by our study, in that women were reluctant to view sexual aggression in strong terms (i.e., rape or coercion or aggression) under romantic or caring circumstances.

As this woman indicates, she put herself in a different category from the other two girls whom her boyfriend forced to have sex. They were raped, she was not:

> I know someone else he done like that. . . . Like he did with me. I didn't
> see it like that [his behavior toward her as rape]. I felt forced but I
> thought I have never been raped before. I did care for him. . . . But I
> didn't want to [have sex] at that time but he made me anyway and he
> enjoyed it. I didn't.

It is a fact that these women who experienced aggression and coercion in their dating relationships tend to use different terminology in describing these episodes than do researchers. Perhaps it is because it is obviously more than a category or abstract event to them. It is a life-defining moment. To label the behavior of a man whom they have dated and cared about as "coercion" or "rape" is to strip away all pretense of equality, reciprocity, and value in the relationship. With this realization, the woman must acknowledge that the "Beast" is not an illusion, and that the "Beauty" is the object of his aggression instead of his love.

Another source of confusion for these women was naïveté. Some women pointed to their dating and sexual inexperience as central to their inability to identify what had happened to them:

> I didn't know anything about date rape. How should I know anything
> about it? I wasn't that involved with anyone!

Some also said that, to the best of their knowledge at the time, such behavior and experiences had no name or label:

> People laugh [now] and say "How could he make you do that?" I say,
> "If you were 14 and you were in a car with someone who had been
> drinking and it was your only ride home, what would you have done?"
> I did not know at the time there was such a thing called "date rape"
> until I came to college and learned about it.

One woman mused about her experiences and beliefs regarding relationships:

> At the time, I didn't know that what was happening to me wasn't happening to everyone else. They could have told me, but I guess it
> wouldn't have made all that much difference. . . . Getting forced to have
> sex, being spoken to in awful terms, and being abused is not normal.

This is a theme that occurs in both the physical and sexual aggression literature with regularity. Even if women come to realize that what happened to them was coercive or worse, they still experience lingering shame and embarrassment. This, in turn, serves to create a self-imposed silence, in which women fear disclosure because of what others will think or because they will be blamed for their poor judgment.

Excusing and Forgiving the Aggressor

One of the first and consistently prevalent tendencies of the women was to describe the aggressors' behaviors in ways that excused them, forgave them, or both. Their rationalization took the form of reference to his family background and gender stereotypes or "doing gender."

Sometimes in the search to explain ongoing aggression, the women began to talk about his family. It was as if his bad experiences from the past could excuse his behavior in their relationship. This woman seeks to explain her partner's behavior:

> I knew that he would probably be violent too because his father had abused his wife for years. And in the end shot her and then shot himself. . . . There was a lot of violence directed toward him [her boyfriend] as a child and so he was the scapegoat of the family. He was placed in foster care for awhile.

One woman described the breakup of a sexually coercive and physically aggressive relationship:

> I told him, "I don't want to see you again, you don't touch me like that." He didn't understand what was wrong. Later I came to find out that he grew up in that type of setting. He thought it was OK to hit a female. . . . That he had to be the controlling figure in the relationship. His father was abusive. If it wasn't in a physical sense, it was in a verbal sense. He grew up in a country town where Mom is supposed to be the barefoot and pregnant type woman.

It seemed that these women's desire to rationalize the aggression based on his family experiences served to divert blame from him and, hence, from her and their relationship. In other words, the cause of the men's aggression was something over which the women had no control. It did not originate with her or the relationship, and although his family experiences were still a source of concern, it was a relief to these women that they were ultimately not responsible for "making him this way."

Perceiving his aggression as part of "just being a man" served as an additional way that the women and those around them excused his aggressive behavior. This is reminiscent of the term "doing gender" used by West and Zimmerman (1991), who expand the concept of gender from a category to a routine or a recurring pattern of behavior: "Doing gender involves a complex of socially guided perceptual, interactional, and micropolitical activities that cast particular pursuits as expressions of masculine and feminine 'natures.'" (p. 14). The women in this study frequently described the behavior of themselves and of the offenders as contextually gendered. Their references to doing gender were multilayered in both complexity and awareness. As women discussed the masculine aspect of doing gender in this situation, they were somewhat baffled by their own and others' defense of his behavior based on this reasoning.

For example, this woman describes her and her mother's attitude toward an early dating experience in which the boy tried to have sex with her when they were on a trip together:

> My mother and I are real close and she even knew about the guy . . . and she really liked him and even she didn't think much about it. I mean, you know, he was just being a boy. It was just kind of laughed off.

The boy, in that situation, was acting within the societal guidelines of masculinity. The woman and her mother responded accordingly, excusing his behavior with the attitude that "boys will be boys."

Another woman disgustedly and angrily described the perspective her offender's friends took of her rape:

> His friends kind of look at it as "Score one for D! Chalk another one up for him!" One of his friends happened to say something like that to my roommate. She told him . . . that if D was still bragging about it, someone needed to talk to him. . . . It seems like small-town people have small-town minds also.

What she described and objected to is the almost automatic acceptance of the abuse of male power and privilege in the sexual arena. Similarly, this woman discussed a cavalier type of male attitude toward sex (representative of many women's thoughts):

> I think there is a pattern there. Those guys tend to think they can get any woman they want no matter what. If they can't, it hurts their pride. So they would be more likely to use force. A bruised ego can make a guy do that. I've seen that.

The women in this study ultimately acknowledged that an attitude or code exists in our society and culture that condones the aggressive and denigrating treatment of women in close relationships. In doing so, they came face to face with the realization of its pervasive impact. For example, this woman talks about her experience when, as an 18-year-old, she filed charges against a fellow Marine after he raped her:

> I took him up on charges with my company. He knew the captain, the CEO; the CEO just couldn't believe that J could do something like that. They investigated somewhat, kind of loose-ended for a couple days. They took statements and depositions. The third day after I reported it I was called in and read my rights. I had been charged with slander and defamation of character. I was told that if I ever brought it up again, I would be court-martialed.

One unfortunate yet common result of women taking public action against their offenders (usually rapists) manifested itself in the form of harassment. After being severely physically and sexually attacked by her boyfriend, this woman faced incredible reactions and harassment from the community:

> I left the town [eventually]. When I went back to the country club where I worked as a bartender, the lawyers and doctors thought it was funny to say things like "Hey, B! How come you didn't tell me all I had to do was bite your nose to get a piece of ass?"

Similar instances were reported as the women discussed the offender's treatment at the hands of other friends, the public, or the legal system. Such experiences in the public arena are not uncommon. Lenient treatment of the offender and a demeaning attitude toward the woman combine in a backlash against the female victim of the aggression, known as victim-blaming.

The Dynamics of Blaming the Victim

This section incorporates a broadly based discussion about the placement of blame on the victim. We begin with a discussion of the dynamics of self-blame and then examine how this self-blame is reinforced by "doing gender" and the victim's feelings of poor judgment. The women at this point discussed these issues with more sophistication and a greater level of understanding than they did when describing their reactions to the aggression.

As we noted in the section on the dynamics of sexual aggression, self-blame was often an immediate response to the aggressive event. These seeds of self-blame did not necessarily erode over time, however; years later, the women still talked about their role in "causing" his aggression and how they felt responsible for placing themselves in "bad situations." This woman blames herself not for the aggression, which occurred when she was 14 years old, but for placing herself in danger:

> He finally left [her house]. I remember just laying there for a while just thinking, "Oh God, what am I going to do now?" At that point I thought, "R, you are so stupid. You shouldn't have let him in." My mother's voice was much louder than anything else. Of course I was not an adult at the time and I didn't have enough insight to realize that it wasn't my fault. I blamed myself for putting myself in a bad situation. Not for the attack, I didn't do that, that was his choice. But "I sure as heck didn't take good care of myself" is the way I thought about it at the time. That I had made a huge mistake.

Self-blame is not a simple issue. Its immediate result is that of excusing the perpetrator's behavior and the revictimization of the woman. Many of the participants in this study talked about taking the responsibility for what happened to them because "they should have known better" or "listened to their mother." Should have known better than what?—To have trusted a boyfriend or acquaintance who had never before acted in an aggressive manner? To have found themselves in uncharted relationship territory? To have trusted friends not to harm them?

This woman describes the situation and her relationship with the man who took her virginity by force. (Later in the interview, she indicated that she took the blame for what happened):

> We were at a party together. We both ended up getting inebriated and it was at his apartment. Everyone left. I guess part of the reason it didn't alarm me was [because] I was pretty drunk so I didn't think about my judgment being altered at all. But I had stayed at his place overnight before and we had never had sex. We had spent time together like that before but I would say "No, I don't want that to happen, period." Whether that meant him crawling on top of me and me pushing him off or me just saying "No, period." But it [the aggression] had never happened before.

As all of these examples indicate, much of the self-blame arises out of having placed oneself in a dangerous or vulnerable situation, due primarily to inexperience in dating. This creates an intriguing paradox in that somewhere young women get the idea that they are almost completely responsible for their own safety in the relationship. It may come from the admonitions of well-meaning yet fearful parents who vehemently warn their daughters about the dangers of dating, of older men, of strangers, and so forth. Yet, if these young women's experience is limited (as with 24% of our sample who were virgins when raped, or 14% who were forced to perform oral sex when virgins), it may be difficult for them to determine from what they should be protecting themselves.

This message, which we see repeated in society through news stories, movies, books, and music, and which comes from parents, may be well-meaning in its attempt to encourage the woman to be proactive rather than a passive victim, but it has a darker side. It "inadvertently" excuses the perpetrator for taking any responsibility for clarifying the ground rules in the relationship (i.e., checking out whether sex is desired) or for his own behavior. The woman's responsibility for communication in the relationship and self-protection has become part of the dominant discourse of courtship. When bad things happen, then, it is a simple matter of logic to shift attention to the woman, the victim, to determine what went wrong. The discourse of aggression emphasizes that these matters are her responsibility. Parents, friends, and family repeat that message, and so women come to accept and believe that the coercion or aggression that happened to them was somehow within their control.

In fact, both Byers's (1996) description of the traditional sexual script and Wetherell's (1995) discussion of the discourse of romanticism explain the potential for sexual coercion. As both authors stated, typically men are seen as the initiators, the asserters of sexual activity, and women as the recipients in the passive role. Furthermore, women are expected to be prepared for this type of behavior and to respond cautiously (Byers, 1996). This reasoning places inexperienced and naive women in a no-win situation, so that if they find themselves in a dangerously coercive situation or are raped, they blame themselves. It becomes part of the romantic discourse and, as such, self-blame is a hidden yet pervasive aspect of the traditional sexual script and of the overarching discourse of courtship.

The ways in which the women felt that their response to his aggression was a part of doing gender bears scrutiny here, as well. In this capacity, women felt they were "doing their job" even though the task was harmful or distasteful. Because these women gave in to powerful messages about the feminine role as well as to his manipulation or force, they felt at least partially responsible for the aggression they experienced. Thus, doing gender served to encourage her to go along with his demands; and, because she went along with him, she must also take some responsibility for his actions. For example, this woman talks about never wanting to have sex with her boyfriend but giving in because he forced her:

> I don't remember thinking "This is horrible, horrible!" But I thought I was doing my job, so to speak.

And this woman talks about being coerced into sexual acts with her boyfriend that she found offensive:

> Usually in the morning we would wake up and he would want to do things . . . and I really didn't want to but being his girlfriend, I gave in.

Previous discussion of the traditional sexual script emphasized the female role as passive. This woman exemplified this in not being able to change her mind or be assertive:

> I felt like I should not have [had sex]. I wanted him to stay after the party. Not to sleep with him [but] just because I enjoyed his company. We were in a room and one thing just led to another. I am just not good at saying no. I guess it would have been wrong if I had said "No."

Some women talk about their poor judgment, still placing some of the blame on themselves. Although not with the same intensity and anguish of earlier discussions, it remains a part of their rationalization process just the same. This woman talks about her experiences:

> I feel like I blame myself because I just get into these predicaments. . . . I've excused it, like "C, you have gotten into this yourself." I know I haven't but when I'm sitting and thinking like I am right now, I really think, "There was H and there was N and then there was A." And I think "How could I have gotten myself in these predicaments three times in a row?"

As a final note, this self-blame extended to subsequent relationships, as well. Several talked about their judgment in terms of a propensity to become involved in harmful relationships. This woman discusses her behavior and self-image as a result of a series of bad sexual experiences that she related to the fact that she was raped at the age of 14:

> It was really hard because I would always blame myself. Anybody victimizes me like that [and] I'd always put it on myself. You know, "You should have done something to prevent it or something." But the first time I really couldn't [and] then I felt I had to play the victim's role.

Reframing the Aggression: Holding the Aggressor Accountable

Nowhere is the effect of the passage of time more evident than in reframing the aggression. In thinking and rethinking the dynamics of the coercion and aggression, the women have come to conclusions that allow them to move on in their lives. Their reasoning and responses have been tempered with education, time, and experience, which give them the insight that was not possible at the time of the aggression.

At times, the women talked about coming to reject their earlier acceptance of traditionally feminine ways of doing gender. They began to recognize the traditional standard that influenced their interactions in these coercive relationships. As this woman expressed, rather indignantly,

> When I think back on it, it was a real power play on his part. He would demand [sex] and I would try not to give in while at the same time make him feel better about it. Feed his ego, I guess, smooth the waters. What nonsense!

Somewhere, it seems, the idea has emerged that men are entitled to sex in the dating exchange. The literature documents that the perception that a woman "owes" a man sex if he takes her out on a date exists in both genders and at a young age (Koss, 1988). Sexual favors from the woman as repayment are part of the discourse of courtship, and attitudes such as this woman describes are common:

> He thought that I had become his, you know, his property and that he had the right to at least try to have sex with me. And I think that he truly believed that if we dated, you know, if he . . . paid for movies, pizzas, spent time with me, that he should have sex with me!

This woman attempted to deal with the issue and failed:

> I just get this sense that when you go out with a guy, he feels you owe him something because maybe he spent money on you. So I started paying my own way when I went out with a guy so I wouldn't get those vibes. But I still got the vibes. I get this feeling [from] all these guys that you're obligated to have sex with them because they took you out. If you don't then something is wrong. This is men my age to early forties. Seems to be a widespread common theme.

A variation of this viewpoint focuses on sexual entitlement after the initial coercion. This woman describes a situation that was reflected in the experiences of several women:

> I remember during that time, several times [that] . . . I didn't feel like sleeping with him and he thought because he had one time [had sex with her] that it gave him rights anytime. I would just lay there because I was crying.

These comments support the supposition that, to a certain extent, the discourse of courtship maintains aspects of the traditional sexual script. Specifically, they explicitly assert the sexual rights of men: the right to initiate sex, the right to ignore a woman's refusal, in sum, the right to sex in a dating relationship (Byers, 1996; Carter, 1995; Metts & Spitzberg, 1996; Muehlenhard & Linton, 1987). Schwartz and DeKeseredy (1997) used the term *courtship patriarchy* to refer to this as a pattern of behavior (i.e., the man is entitled to sex and, if refused, is entitled to use force to get it). When these "rights" were acted on, we have seen that they had enormous psychological consequences for women. An important part of recovery from the aggressive experience became the rejection of this discourse and the recognition of the impact that it had on how they had erroneously framed the aggression as their own fault.

❧ A Final Note

At the beginning of these two studies, we had no preconceived notions regarding our findings other than viewing them through the lenses we outlined in Chapter 2. Although the experiences of the women in these two studies were diverse, there were similarities. For example, the catalysts for the aggression, control, and the victims' response of self-blame were strong recurring themes. Also, in their attempts to deal with the aftermath of aggression, all women talked of their initial shock, fear, and disbelief.

The reactions of the aggressors were also similar in both studies when they responded as if nothing had happened. However, some physically abusive men begged forgiveness, whereas other sexually aggressive men expressed anger. Perhaps one of the major differences between the studies deals with definitional issues. Physically assaulted women appeared to have less trouble labeling their experience as such. Sexually assaulted women, however, expressed considerable confusion and difficulty in dealing with their experience based on their lack of a sufficient definition of the event.

Both sets of women excused the aggression, citing the aggressor's family background and highlighting their own behavior as contributing to the aggression. Finally, they reframed the aggression in very different ways. When physically abused women's perceptions changed, they left the relationship. When sexually abused women's perceptions changed, they became more cautious in dealing with men and dating.

Perhaps the most positive aspect of both studies is the obvious courage and resilience these women showed. As very young women, they faced stressful, dangerous, and traumatic circumstances with strength and determination. These women experienced adversity and took pride in that they moved past it, gaining strength from having worked through a terrible experience.

The women of this study documented for us their process of constructing meaning from their personal chaos. The meaning works for them, for the most part, because it has to work. It is not up to researchers or readers to judge the conclusions they drew or the pathways their reasoning took but rather to examine their words to understand how these women constructed meaning from trauma.

5

❦

Conclusions and Implications for Intervention

This final chapter has two main purposes. First, based on our findings in these two studies and on the literature, we present a series of conclusions about the dynamics and effects of physical and sexual aggression during dating and courtship. Second, we address possible avenues of intervention and prevention. In both sections of this chapter, we frame our conclusions in the form of working statements; in this way, we hope to highlight the major insights gained in this qualitative study as well as the ways in which our work is tied to that of many other scholars and activists. Our use of the term "working" statements is purposeful, for we emphasize the ongoing nature of our inquiry into this topic and our openness to modify each hypothesis as new insights unfold.

ಶ Conclusions About Aggression in Courtship

The conclusions that we draw from our research can all be related to the overarching concept of discourses. It is specifically the discourses of courtship and violence that are reflected in the ways in which young women construct sense out of their experiences.

The women in these studies talked of their experiences within the dominant discourses of society. They described their courtship and dating in terms of power and control and articulated their versions of the myth of equality between the sexes. They described how ideals of romance influenced their decisions about relationships as well as how sexuality became intertwined with emotions, control, and aggression. In discussing violence, they struggled with excusing the aggressor versus blaming themselves and coped with the reactions of others. The women in these studies labored to define their experiences as aggression and struggled with the invisible nature of aggression in the dating culture and in our society. In the working statements that follow, we identify and reflect on each of these concepts in greater detail.

Most Young Women Believe Aggression Will
Never Happen in Their Relationships

A clear sense of disbelief pervaded the narratives provided by the young women who had experienced physical and sexual aggression. The first time aggression happened, each woman experienced shock, disbelief, and confusion. Not only did she report not knowing how to feel about the aggression she had experienced, she also reported that she did not even know how to define it. Was this experience physical *abuse*? Was it *rape*? What was it if intercourse did not occur? Was there a name for what happened to her? And how could she make sense of this experience, given that this man was not a stranger, she never saw him (before this incident) as hateful or harmful, and he said that he loved her? How could this awful experience fit into the context of a loving and close relationship?

We believe that the dominant discourse of courtship simply does not allow the construction of a close and intimate relationship to include physical violence and sexual aggression. Harm at the hands of one you love is just not a part of this fairy tale. Despite the widespread attention given to sensational cases of intimate violence and date rape in the past decade, there remains a pervasive sense that this is something that happens to other people (an integral part of the discourse of aggression, for it is always "another" who is constructed as the victim of violent actions). Thus, both the discourse of courtship and the discourse of aggression contribute to a construction of relationships and aggression as antithetical, at least in *my* relationship.

Control Is a Key Dynamic in Both Physical and Sexual Aggression

As noted in the conceptual framework that we presented in Chapter 2, we began our analysis of the narratives with a framework that highlighted the ways in which aggression is connected to issues of control. After poring over the transcripts many times and engaging in many converging conversations about coding the data, we were struck again and again by the ways in which issues of control pervaded the women's narratives. A cynic would declare that we simply found what we were looking for. We think such a criticism would be too simplistic, however. Rather, we attempted to be clear and up-front about the lenses through which we would examine the data. In addition, we found the references to men's control-based motivations to be interwoven throughout each narrative in multiple and complex ways, confirming the work of other scholars which emphasizes that control is integral to understanding the dynamics of both physical and sexual aggression.

This is not to say that control is the only dynamic that is noteworthy. Some of the women who experienced physical aggression simultaneously described a dynamic of expressive violence; their partners were described as unpredictable, as having volatile tempers, as men who were ready to explode at the least perceived provocation or violation of a relational rule. The women who described their experiences of sexual aggression were clear about the role of the men's sexual desire in a context in which they felt it was appropriate to exert their sexual rights through force, coercion, or both. Thus, both samples of women spoke about how control dynamics were interwoven with these issues of emotional expressiveness and sexual desire. Ultimately, their meaning-making around these incidents of aggression included the construction of control as a key underlying dynamic of physical and sexual aggression.

It is evident to us that we need to understand the broad and complex span of power relations as they determine the construction of behavior and meaning. Instead of a limited focus on singular sources and aspects of power and control, it is necessary to examine these issues as they relate to patriarchy, gender, the family, the aggression itself, and sexuality. Only when power—and control—are approached as interactive and overarching concepts will we be able to address effectively the dynamics of aggression in intimate relationships.

Aggression Intersects With Interpersonal Communication on Multiple Levels

Another key variable in understanding the dynamics and impact of physical and sexual aggression are patterns of interpersonal communication. The women who experienced physical aggression provided many cogent examples of how communication dynamics played into the precipitation of a violent episode; physical aggression was framed as the result of a conflict that escalated out of control, as a result of ineffective patterns of communication, and as tied to verbal and emotional coercion. The women who experienced sexual aggression also spoke of the role of communication dynamics, including misperceived cues, interpreting women's "no" as a token refusal, and purposely ignoring her protests.

However, the communication dynamics of physical and sexual aggression do not stop with the analysis of the aggressive incident itself. They also are apparent in two additional ways. First, many of these young women found it difficult, even impossible, to talk about what had happened to them with the perpetrator, with their friends, with their families, and, most certainly, with formal intervention systems. This difficulty arose from the sensitive and intimate nature of what had happened, the difficulty of labeling the aggression as abuse or rape, and the bizarre and potentially dangerous situation of trying to talk things over with the person who hurt them (who also may have refused to talk about or acknowledge his actions).

Another area in which interpersonal communication dynamics are integral is in the process of constructing meaning. Often, shifts in the meaning of his aggressive actions occurred in a social context: the remark of a friend that "a real man would never hit a woman," or a conversation with a family member that framed his forced sexual intimacy as rape. For many women, this construction of the reality of their own experience slowly materialized after conversations with friends, teachers, colleagues, or family members, conversations possibly about personal experiences but more likely within the context of a discussion about a news story, movie, book, or topic in the classroom. If they were lucky, they found someone to listen, someone who cared and understood. If they were not, they continued to carry their burden alone.

Victims of Physical and Sexual Aggression Are Silenced in Multiple Ways

Silencing occurs at all levels of a victim's experience. Personally, she can hardly find the words to describe what happened to her. The language simply does not exist that can articulate her physical and emotional experiences. (If the discourse of courtship does not recognize physical and sexual aggression within intimate relationships, how can she speak of it?) In addition, as discussed in the previous section, she is silenced by embarrassment, the sensitivity of the topic, fear of others' (particularly family members') reactions, and/or others' inability or unwillingness to listen.

Perhaps the most insidious form of silencing that these young women experience comes from the intervention system, primarily the legal system. When women file charges, there are various results. We have seen that, unfortunately, many women become gravely disappointed in the system that lets the aggressor go, imposes perfunctory penalties, and cannot or will not protect her from her aggressor. She eventually is left with a sense of helplessness, in that she could not effect change, and hopelessness regarding men and the system as a whole. All in all, these are extremely effective methods of silencing the problem.

Is it any wonder that many women "never told" about their physical or sexual abuse? They cited many reasons, including shame, self-blame, inexperience, and ignorance, but the bottom line is that if our society took seriously its responsibility for the vulnerable, there would be no need for silence. The aggression, whether physical or sexual, is the dark side of the dominant discourse of courtship. Within courtship, women are denied a voice with which to identify and detail the existence of aggression, and, as such, aggression has become a hidden aspect of many women's lives for lack of support, a forum for discussion, or both. It is the accumulation of "deaf ears" that ultimately results in muting the pain and denying the event.

A Sense of Betrayal and Self-Blame Are
Pervasive Effects of Experiencing Aggression

The women whom we interviewed spoke of myriad effects of the abuse that they experienced, including insomnia, fear of men, lost confidence, feelings of worthlessness, anger and rage, withdrawal from family and friends, repression of the details of the event, inability to enjoy sex, promiscuity, and depression. Not too surprisingly, 39% of the sample of women who had experienced sexual aggression were in counseling; the vast majority of the women in both samples reported deep mistrust of men and hesitation in getting romantically or sexually involved again for several years after the aggressive relationship had ended. Certainly, the impact of experiencing aggression at the hands of someone they thought cared about them threaded its way through many facets of these women's lives for many years.

Two arenas of impact were particularly noteworthy in the narratives. First, the women relayed a deep sense of betrayal. This sense of betrayal extended way beyond the betrayal inherent in their relationships with the men who abused them to encompass a feeling that friends and family had betrayed them by not protecting them. They also felt that society had betrayed them by not providing adequate means for punishing the aggressor and, in the case of sexual aggression, by even condoning the sexual assault or coercion.

This sense of betrayal also extended to a betrayal of her innocence; one young woman commented that after all she had been through in her relationship with a severely abusive man, she "never felt like a teenager again"—she had seen and experienced too much that her age mates simply could not fathom. Still others spoke about the ways in which their naïveté had been shattered and their open acceptance of people changed forever. Ultimately, their vision for relationships was crushed, leading some to conclude that "that's just the way relationships are."

The second arena of impact that spoke clearly within the narratives was self-blame. As we highlighted in Chapters 3 and 4, blaming the victim and excusing the aggressor were integral components of trying to figure out what had happened. As such, self-blame represents two connected and strangely complementary aspects of constructing meaning, for within that process responsibility for the aggression has to be assigned. Therefore, if responsibility does not reside with the aggressor, it must be the responsibility of the victim. Obviously, this is an oversimplification of the dynamics of a lengthy process, our point being that the victims find and struggle with the "gray" area in a supposedly straightforward scenario. They discussed at length factors that could excuse his behavior such as a poor or violent family background, societal values that support his use of force, the influence of his friends on his drinking, attitudes toward women or violence, "doing gender," and the like. At the same time, they identified numerous ways of placing blame for the aggression squarely at their own feet: They should have known better than to put themselves in that situation, they were blind for not being able to "see the signs" of violence, they "egged him on" until he hit, or they led him on or did not say "no" strongly enough.

Perhaps excusing the abuser and blaming the victim are so interwoven because ultimately we reflect the views of the society in which we live. In a patriarchal society and, hence, courtship system, sexual and physical aggression are forms of controlling women. The pièce de resistance of control, then, is to place the blame for that aggression on the victim. In reality, we know, and the women came to believe over time and healing, that the aggression was not their responsibility, but that of the perpetrator who chose to behave in an aggressive manner.

Women Who Survive Physical and Sexual Aggression Display Insight and Resiliency

As a final note to our observations across all the interviews, we emphasize the incredible strengths displayed by the women we interviewed. When we asked them about the impact of this experience on their lives, the women did not always speak solely of negative effects. They also talked about the ways in which they were taking action to repair their lives and sense of agency. They spoke of increased independence, of new sensitivity to signs of control in a dating partner, and of having walked away from subsequent relationships when even the hint of control or aggression surfaced.

They talked about the ways in which a relationship with a therapist, with parents and friends, and/or with a new (nonabusive) romantic partner helped heal their trust in their own judgment and in intimacy. With time and support, their resiliency enabled them to draw strength from what happened to them to reframe their perspectives of themselves and their relationships with others. Their advice to other women was to believe in and stand up for yourself, and for men to have respect for and listen to women. Over and over in the interviews, we heard these women state that if they could help keep other women and men from getting into aggressive situations, then perhaps some good would come of their experiences after all. These young women were fortunate, for they found people who listened, people to whom they could talk. Many women do not.

ੈ Implications for Intervention

We conclude this chapter with a brief discussion of implications for intervention and prevention. Here, we draw on the excellent insights in the article by Rosen and Stith (1993) on intervention with women who have been abused. We do not attempt to address all possible arenas of intervention; rather, we conclude with a few remarks about the areas that seemed to flow most naturally from our findings in the two studies.

First, Rosen and Stith (1993) highlighted the importance of taking a strong stand against aggression within the therapeutic setting. Aggression should not be minimized, and concerns for a client's safety should be openly discussed. We would add that this type of framing of the situation is just as important for less formal interventions, from the conversation that a teacher might have with a teenager to the support offered by friend. Certainly, the results of this study support the importance of framing physically and sexually aggressive behavior as abusive and wrong. The women we interviewed talked about their search for meaning around the aggression that had occurred and the struggle to define his behavior, marked by questions such as "Was it abuse?" and "Was it not really his fault?" Clearly, conversations—with both informal and formal support people—that help the young woman who has been victimized to frame her experience as abuse and as inappropriate, undeserved behavior can do a great deal to ameliorate the self-blame that all too often surrounds aggression.

Second, again following the lead of Rosen and Stith (1993), we emphasize the importance of understanding why a young woman might choose to stay with an abusive partner. Given the incredible pressure to be "partnered" and the many ways that the discourse of courtship capitalizes on the positive side of courtship (and virtually ignores anything that might be nonegalitarian or nonromantic), it is not surprising that aggression that occurs in the context of an already established relationship does not immediately lead to the demise of the relationship. Indeed, as our results have demonstrated, the process of forgiving the aggressor and blaming oneself can lead to a spiral of self-doubt from which it is very difficult to extricate oneself. Both Rosen (1996) and Kirkwood (1993) eloquently described the processes of seduction and entrapment that make it so very difficult to end the relationship with the abuser. As Rosen and Stith noted, it is important to not lay further blame on the victim by emphasizing that she should or must leave, if her decision is to stay. At the same time, Rosen and Stith believed that it is important to help the woman consider leaving. They suggested developing a safety plan, using future-oriented presuppositional questions about when she might know that his apologies are not enough, how she will know that it is time to move on, and helping clients listen to their inner "warning voices."

Our third suggestion for intervention is to address the importance of working through issues of self-blame and help the victim reframe physical and sexual aggression in terms of the aggressor's responsibility. This is an important goal, not only for intervention with young women who are still in a relationship with the aggressor, but also for young women who have exited their relationships. Our results demonstrated that strong feelings of self-blame and self-doubt remained with the young women for years afterward. Working through these feelings may be critical for rebuilding a sense of agency, self-confidence, and ability to protect oneself.

Fourth, we emphasize the importance of paying attention to what often are construed as "minor" incidents of aggression, in the hopes of preventing escalated and severe aggression. Even when the women we interviewed were describing what might be defined as minor aggression (e.g., pushing, shoving, verbal pressure to have sex), they still described chilling patterns of control, coercion, and presumed male rights. We speculate that the seeds of severe battering and sexual aggression can be sown very early in a relationship and that issues of patriarchal terrorism (see Johnson, 1995) can arise long before a legal commitment of marriage is made.

Ultimately, we emphasize the importance of elevating subordinate (and competing) discourses of aggression and courtship (Gavey, 1996). This alternative discourse would emphasize the importance of paying attention to warning signs such as controlling behavior and "minor" aggression. It would hold aggressors accountable. It would go beyond the "myth of equality" to emphasize the rights of both women and men to truly egalitarian relationships. And it would celebrate women's successful resistance to aggression, their strength, their independence, and their agency (Gavey, 1996).

Finally, we direct attention to the responsibility of society regarding the treatment and study of relationship violence. We assert that the influence of societal discourses on dating and relationship aggression is vast and complex. Social institutions such as the legal system, family, government, medicine, and the welfare system provide the foundation of power for discourses. These institutions exist within and perpetuate a patriarchal structure that has been shown to silence and marginalize victims of aggression. The prevalent societal response to victims and abusers, then, has been to provide partial solutions within an obscurant system rife with obstacles. What is needed, instead, is a constructivistic, integrative response to treat both the individuals who experience aggression and the aggression itself. We propose that the first step in this reformation involves society recognizing those aspects of its discourses of gender and courtship that support aggression. Only when we begin to address the value structures that shape the dynamics of aggression in relationships will interventions be effective.

❧ A Final Note of Thanks

In closing, we sincerely thank each of the young women who shared their lives with us. We have come to define our role in this phase of the research as, in part, a stewardship in which we were entrusted with their experiences and stories. It clearly was not easy or pleasant for them to talk at length about these issues with virtual strangers. Yet, they found the courage to do so, and it is our responsibility to honor them by representing their stories with sensitivity and compassion. In doing so, we hope that professionals, students, family and friends, and future intimate partners of the women who have experienced aggression will gain greater insight into the complex problems of physical and sexual aggression in dating relationships.

In wrapping up the interviews, we asked if the women had anything to add. Janet said she had one concern about the interview, and, thinking that she wanted to ensure her anonymity, I prepared to reiterate how that would be accomplished. Instead, she haltingly explained how she had worried about becoming part of the study because of how I might feel about her after hearing her story. She asked if I thought differently or badly of her. I remember feeling stunned, wholly inadequate, and wondering what showed on my face. I asked myself "What would an objective researcher say now?" Nothing came to mind. I looked across at the beautiful young woman who had been in my classes and who had endured such physical and emotional trauma and felt a flood of emotion quite unlike anything I had ever felt before. The uncertainty in her eyes demanded a "subjective" response. I put my arm around her and told her that I thought she was an articulate, complex, sensitive, and courageous person. Sometime later, I realized the irony of the situation. Her question had come at the end of a 2-hour interview filled with difficult and extremely personal questions, all directed at her. With that one simple question, however, she changed my professional and personal lives forever.

Appendix A

Physical Aggression Interview Protocol

1. Tell me a little about your relationship with _____.

   Where did you meet?

   Are you still together? If not, when did the relationship end?

   How long did you date (or have you been dating)?

   What first attracted you to _____?

2. Now I am going to ask you about physical aggression in this relationship. First, who usually started it when hitting occurred?

   Tell me how many times your partner did each of the following during your relationship:

   Threatened to hit or throw something at you

   Threw or smashed or kicked something

   Threw something at you

   Pushed, grabbed, or shoved you

   Slapped you on the face

   Slapped you on the body

   Kicked, bit, or hit with a fist

Hit or tried to hit you with an object

Choked you

Beat you up

Threatened you with, or used, a knife or gun

Now, please tell me how often you did each of the following: (repeat behaviors listed above)

Did any of these behaviors (see above) ever happen when you were growing up? That is, did your mom or dad ever hit you, slap you, kick, hit with an object, etc.? (please be specific)

Did your mom or dad ever act this way to one of your brothers or sisters?

Did your mom and dad ever act aggressively toward one another?

How about brothers and sisters?

3. Please describe to me the first time aggression occurred in your relationship. Tell me what led up to the violence, how you reacted, and what happened afterward. (Probe for detail here.)

4. Now please describe the most recent incident of aggression.

5. When _____ hit you, what do you think he hoped to accomplish? In other words, why did he hit you?

6. When you hit _____, what did you hope to accomplish? Why did you hit him?

   Or—Why didn't you ever hit _____ back?

7. In this relationship, how did you go about getting what you wanted from _____? Did you talk, cry, pout, discuss, or what?

8. How does the fact that you were in a violent relationship affect you now? For example, does it make you scared of involvement? (Try not to lead the interviewee here.)

INTERVIEWERS: Thank them very much and reassure them that their information will be used to help other women who have had similar experiences and to hopefully prevent such things from happening to others! This research eventually will take the form of a book on "physical aggression in dating relationships."

If anyone asks for help in dealing with her experiences, you may refer them to J, a counselor in the guidance center here on campus. If the respondent is not a student, refer her to _____ [a community mental health agency and a local shelter].

Appendix B

Sexual Aggression Interview Protocol

1. You have just answered a survey that asked for a lot of detail about your experience with sexual aggression. I'm interested in your story of what happened. Tell me a little about your relationship with _____. Where did you meet? Did you date? If so, how long did you date (or have you been dating)? (How long ago did you break up?) What first attracted you to _____?

2. Now, please describe to me the first time that sexual aggression occurred. I want to know the whole sequence of events. In other words, tell me what led up to it (what you were doing), how you reacted, and what happened afterward. PROBE QUESTIONS: Where did it happen? His or your place, car, dorm, etc. Were others around? What were you doing prior to the aggression? What did he do and/or say afterward?

3. Did you tell anyone what happened (friend, parents, teacher, counselor, go to a rape crisis center)? What were their reactions?

4. Did you see this coming (did you suspect that he would do this)? Were you surprised? Looking at it now, was there a pattern that led up to or something that triggered the aggression?

5. When he assaulted you, what do you think he hoped to accomplish? (What made him have to use force or convince you?)

6. (If appropriate) Tell me about the last incident of sexual aggression or violence.

7. Sometimes we wonder how these types of behaviors can continue to occur, and I think that part of the reason is because of attitudes. We can and do rationalize a lot of things that happen to us. In that vein, I want you to think about the list of behaviors that I'm going to read and tell me if you think they could be justified in any of your relationships and under what conditions. And think about whether they could be justified on a broader level in our society (are there people out there who might say that under certain circumstances they could see how these things might happen?).

     Sexual contact by verbal coercion (talk you into it)

     Sexual contact by misuse of authority

     Sexual contact by threat

     Attempted intercourse by threat or force

     Attempted intercourse by alcohol or drugs

     Intercourse by verbal coercion

     Intercourse by misuse of authority

     Intercourse by alcohol or drugs

     Intercourse by threat or force

     Oral/anal penetration by threat or force

8. Did any physical aggression occur in this relationship? In any other relationship? (If "yes," repeat list of behaviors for each relationship—for "partner," "you," and "his parents." Continue with questions through Number 11, except "most recent incidence of aggression." If "no," skip to Number 11.)

9. I'm going to ask you some questions with regard to the physical aggression in your relationship. First, who usually started it when the hitting occurred?

10. Tell me how many times your partner did each of the following during your relationship:

Threatened to hit or throw something at you

Threw or smashed or kicked something

Threw something at you

Pushed, grabbed, or shoved you

Slapped you on the face

Slapped you on the body

Kicked, bit, or hit with a fist

Hit or tried to hit you with an object

Choked you

Beat you up

Threatened you with a gun or knife

Used a gun or knife on you

Now tell me how often you did each of the following: (repeat behaviors)

11. Did your parents ever do these things to each other? (repeat list, if necessary) Did your partner's parents ever do these things to each other? (repeat list, if necessary) Did your parents ever do these things to you or a sibling? (repeat list, if necessary) Did your partner's parents ever do these things to him or a sibling? (repeat list, if necessary)

12. Please describe to me the first time physical aggression occurred in your relationship with _____. Tell me what led up to it, how you reacted, and what happened afterward.

13. Did you see it coming? Was there a pattern that would lead up to the aggression or something that would trigger the violent episodes? Please describe the most recent incidence of physical aggression.

14. When _____ hit you, what do you think he was hoping to accomplish? (Whichever is appropriate:) When you hit him, what were you trying to accomplish? Why didn't you hit him back?

15. How does the fact that you experienced this sexual aggression affect you and how you deal with relationships now? (Also physical aggression, if applicable—Be sure they delineate between the effects as to whether they were physical or sexual outcomes.)

16. Do you expect to experience these behaviors in other dating relationships? (Probe: Expectations for themselves and their own behavior in dating relationships—Are they different? How? Expectations for dating partners?) Effects on friendships (expectations, behaviors—for self and friends)? Effects on relationships with family members (expectations, behaviors—for self and family)?

17. If you could help your younger brother or sister or a child, what would you change about dating relationships?

18. Do you have anything else to add or any comments about the interview? (They may continue on. Let them get things off their chest. There may be something that they have thought about and want to elaborate on.) You may repeat this question several times. Let them end the interview when possible (time or getting off track may be exceptions to the rule).

INTERVIEWERS: Thank them very much and reassure them that their information will be used to help other women who have had similar experiences and to hopefully prevent such things from happening to others! This research eventually will take the form of a book on "sexual and physical aggression in dating relationships."

If anyone asks for help in dealing with her experiences, you may refer them to J, a counselor in the guidance center here on campus. If the respondent is not a student, refer her to _____.

References

Abbey, A., Ross, L. T., McGuffie, D., & McAuslan, P. (1996). Alcohol and dating risk factors for sexual assault among college women. *Psychology of Women Quarterly, 20*, 147-169.

Abma, J., Driscoll, A., & Moore, K. (1998). Young women's degree of control over first intercourse: An exploratory analysis. *Family Planning Perspectives, 30*, 12-18.

Allen, K. R. (1989). *Single women/family ties: Life histories of older women.* Newbury Park, CA: Sage.

Amick, A. E., & Calhoun, K. S. (1987). Resistance to sexual aggression: Personality, attitudinal and situational factors. *Archives of Sexual Behavior, 16*, 153-163.

Anglin, K., & Holtzworth-Munroe, A. (1997). Comparing the responses of maritally violent and nonviolent spouses to problematic marital and nonmarital situations: Are the skills deficits of physically aggressive husbands and wives global? *Journal of Family Psychology, 11*, 301-313.

Arias, I., Samios, M., & O'Leary, K. D. (1987). Prevalence and correlates of physical aggression during courtship. *Journal of Interpersonal Violence, 2*, 82-90.

Avni, N. (1991a). Battered wives: Characteristics of their courtship days. *Journal of Interpersonal Violence, 6*, 232-239.

Avni, N. (1991b). Battered wives: The home as a total institution. *Violence and Victims, 6*, 137-149.

Baber, K. M., & Allen, K. R. (1992). *Women & families: Feminist reconstructions.* New York: Guilford.

Barnes, G. E., Greenwood, L., & Sommer, R. (1991). Courtship violence in a Canadian sample of male college students. *Family Relations, 40,* 37-44.

Barnett, O. W., & LaViolette, A. D. (1993). *It could happen to anyone: Why battered women stay.* Newbury Park, CA: Sage.

Barnett, O. W., Miller-Perrin, C. L., & Perrin, R. D. (1997). *Family violence across the life span.* Thousand Oaks, CA: Sage.

Bartle, S. E., & Rosen, K. (1994). Individuation and relationship violence. *American Journal of Family Therapy, 22,* 222-236.

Belknap, J. (1989). The sexual victimization of unmarried women by nonrelative acquaintances. In M. A. Pirog-Good & J. E. Stets (Eds.), *Violence in dating relationships: Emerging social issues* (pp. 205-218). New York: Praeger.

Beneke, T. (1982). *Men on rape.* New York: St. Martin's Press.

Berger, P. L., & Kellner, H. (1970). Marriage and the construction of reality. In H. P. Dreitzel (Ed.), *Recent sociology* (No. 2, pp. 50-72). New York: Macmillan.

Bergman, L. (1992). Dating violence among high school students. *Social Work, 37,* 21-27.

Bernard, J. (1987). Reviewing the impact of women's studies on sociology. In C. Farnham (Ed.), *The impact of feminist research in the academy* (pp. 193-216). Bloomington: Indiana University Press.

Bird, G. W., Stith, S. M., & Schladale, J. (1991). Psychological resources, coping strategies, and negotiation styles as discriminators of violence in dating relationships. *Family Relations, 40,* 45-50.

Blixeth, E. D. (1987). *Uncharged battery.* New York: Warner.

Bograd, M. (1984). Family systems approaches to wife battering: A feminist critique. *American Journal of Orthopsychiatry, 54,* 558-568.

Bograd, M. (1988). Feminist perspectives on wife abuse: An introduction. In K. Yllö & M. Bograd (Eds.), *Feminist perspectives on wife abuse* (pp. 11-27). Newbury Park, CA: Sage.

Bograd, M. (1990). Why we need gender to understand human violence. *Journal of Interpersonal Violence, 5,* 132-135.

Bookwala, J., Frieze, I. H., Smith, C., & Ryan, K. (1992). Predictors of dating violence: A multivariate analysis. *Violence and Victims, 7,* 297-311.

Bookwala, J., & Zdaniuk, B. (1998). Adult attachment styles and aggressive behavior within dating relationships. *Journal of Social and Personal Relationships, 15,* 175-190.

Boswell, A. A., & Spade, J. Z. (1996). Fraternities and collegiate rape culture: Why are some fraternities more dangerous places for women? *Gender & Society, 10,* 133-147.

Bradbury, T., & Lawrence, E. (1999). Physical aggression and the longitudinal course of newlywed marriage. In X. B. Arriaga & S. Oskamp (Eds.), *Violence in intimate relationships* (pp. 181-202). Thousand Oaks, CA: Sage.

Breines, W., & Gordon, L. (1983). The new scholarship on family violence. *Signs, 8,* 490-531.

Breitenbecher, K. H., & Gidycz, C. A. (1998). An empirical evaluation of a program designed to reduce the risk of multiple sexual victimization. *Journal of Interpersonal Violence, 4*, 472-488.

Browne, A. (1993). Violence against women by male partners: Prevalence, outcomes, and policy implications. *American Psychologist, 48*, 1077-1087.

Brownmiller, S. (1975). *Against our will: Men, women and rape.* New York: Simon & Schuster.

Burcky, W., Reuterman, N., & Kopsky, S. (1988). Dating violence among high school students. *School Counselor, 35*, 353-358.

Burke, P. J., Stets, J. E., & Pirog-Good, M. A. (1989). Gender identity, self esteem, and physical and sexual abuse in dating relationships. In M. A. Pirog-Good & J. E. Stets (Eds.), *Violence in dating relationships: Emerging social issues* (pp. 72-93). New York: Praeger.

Burkhart, B. R., & Stanton, A. L. (1988). Sexual aggression in acquaintance relationships. In G. W. Russell (Ed.), *Violence in intimate relationships* (pp. 43-65). New York: PMA.

Burman, B., John, R. S., & Margolin, G. (1992). Observed patterns of conflict in violent, nonviolent and nondistressed couples. *Behavioral Assessment, 14*, 15-37.

Burman, B., Margolin, G., & John, R. S. (1993). America's angriest home videos: Behavioral contingencies observed in home reenactments of marital conflict. *Journal of Consulting and Clinical Psychology, 61*, 28-39.

Byers, E. S. (1996). How well does the traditional sexual script explain sexual coercion? Review of a program of research. In E. S. Byers & L. F. O'Sullivan (Eds.), *Sexual coercion in dating relationships* (pp. 7-25). New York: Hawthorne.

Byers, E. S., Giles, B. L., & Price, D. L. (1987). Definiteness and effectiveness of women's responses to unwanted sexual advances: A laboratory investigation. *Basic and Applied Social Psychology, 8*, 321-338.

Cahn, D. D. (1996). Family violence from a communication perspective. In D. D. Cahn & S. A. Lloyd (Eds.), *Family violence from a communication perspective* (pp. 1-19). Thousand Oaks, CA: Sage.

Calhoun, K. S., Bernat, J. A., Clum, G. A., & Frame, C. L. (1997). Sexual coercion and attraction to sexual aggression in a community sample of young men. *Journal of Interpersonal Violence, 12*, 392-406.

Campbell, A. (1993). *Men, women and aggression.* New York: Basic Books.

Canterbury, R. J., Grossman, S. J., & Lloyd, E. (1993). Drinking behaviors and lifetime incidence of date rape among high school graduates upon entering college. *College Student Journal, 27*, 75-84.

Carey, C. M., & Mongeau, P. A. (1996). Communication and violence in courtship relationships. In D. D. Cahn & S. A. Lloyd (Eds.), *Family violence from a communication perspective* (pp. 127-150). Thousand Oaks, CA: Sage.

Carlson, B. E. (1996). Dating violence: Student beliefs about consequences. *Journal of Interpersonal Violence, 11*, 3-18.

Carlson, B. E. (1997). A stress and coping approach to intervention with abused women. *Family Relations, 46*, 291-298.

Carter, C. (1995). Introduction. In C. Carter (Ed.), *The other side of silence: Women tell about their experiences with date rape* (pp. 7-22). Gilsum, NH: Avocus.

Cate, R. M., Henton, J. M., Koval, J. E., Christopher, F. S., & Lloyd, S. A. (1982). Premarital abuse: A social psychological perspective. *Journal of Family Issues, 3*, 79-90.

Cate, R. M., & Lloyd, S. A. (1992). *Courtship*. Newbury Park, CA: Sage.

Check, J. P., & Malamuth, N. M. (1983). Sex role stereotyping and reactions to depictions of stranger versus acquaintance rape. *Journal of Personality and Social Psychology, 45*, 344-356.

Christopher, F. S. (1988). An initial investigation into a continuum of premarital sexual pressure. *Journal of Sex Research, 25*, 255-266.

Christopher, F. S., Madura, M., & Weaver, L. (1998). Premarital sexual aggressors: A multivariate analysis of social, relational, and individual variables. *Journal of Marriage and the Family, 60*, 56-69.

Christopher, F. S., Owens, L. A., & Strecker, H. L. (1993). Exploring the dark side of courtship: A test of a model of male premarital sexual aggression. *Journal of Marriage and the Family, 55*, 469-479.

Coan, J., Gottman, J. M., Babcock, J., & Jacobson, N. (1997). Battering and the male rejection of influence from women. *Aggressive Behavior, 23*, 375-388.

Coffey, P., Leitenberg, H., Henning, K., Bennett, R. T., & Jankowski, M. K. (1996). Dating violence: The association between methods of coping and women's psychological adjustment. *Violence and Victims, 11*, 227-238.

Cook, S. L. (1995). Acceptance and expectation of sexual aggression in college students. *Psychology of Women Quarterly, 19*, 181-194.

Coontz, S. (1992). *The way we never were: American families and the nostalgia trap*. New York: Basic Books.

Copenhaver, S., & Grauerholz, E. (1991). Sexual victimization among sorority women: Exploring the link between sexual violence and institutional practices. *Sex Roles, 24*, 31-41.

Currie, D. (1998). Violent men or violent women? Whose definition counts? In R. K. Bergen (Ed.), *Issues in intimate violence* (pp. 97-111). Thousand Oaks, CA: Sage.

Deal, J. E., & Wampler, K. (1986). Dating violence: The primacy of previous experience. *Journal of Social and Personal Relationships, 3*, 457-471.

DeKeseredy, W. S. (1988). *Woman abuse in dating relationships: The role of male peer support*. Toronto, Canada: Canadian Scholars' Press.

DeKeseredy, W. S. (1990). Woman abuse in dating relationships: The contribution of male peer support. *Sociological Inquiry, 60*, 236-243.

DeKeseredy, W. S., Saunders, D. G., Schwartz, M. D., & Alvi, S. (1997). The meanings and motives for women's use of violence in Canadian college

dating relationships: Results from a national survey. *Sociological Spectrum,*
17, 199-222.

DeKeseredy, W. S., & Schwartz, M. D. (1998). *Woman abuse on campus: Results
from the Canadian national survey.* Thousand Oaks, CA: Sage.

Delanty, G. (1997). *Social science: Beyond constructivism and realism.* Minneapolis: University of Minnesota Press.

Dell, P. F. (1989). Violence and the systemic view: The problem of power. *Family Process, 28,* 1-14.

DiLorio, J. A. (1989). Being and becoming coupled: The emergence of female
subordination in heterosexual relationships. In B. J. Risman & P. Schwartz
(Eds.), *Gender in intimate relationships* (pp. 94-104). Belmont, CA: Wads-
worth.

Dobash, R. E., & Dobash, R. P. (1979). *Violence against wives: A case against patriarchy.* New York: Free Press.

Dobash, R. P., Dobash, R. E., Wilson, M., & Daly, M. (1992). The myth of sexual
symmetry in marital violence. *Social Problems, 39,* 71-91.

Drout, C., Becker, T., Bukkosy, S., & Mansell, M. (1994). Does social influence
mitigate or exacerbate responsibility for rape. *Journal of Social Behavior and
Personality, 9,* 409-420.

Dutton, D. G. (1988). *The domestic assault of women.* Boston: Allyn & Bacon.

Dutton, D. G., & Browning, S. J. (1988). Power struggles and intimacy anxie-
ties as causative factors of violence in intimate relationships. In G. Russell
(Ed.), *Violence in intimate relationships* (pp. 163-176). Newbury Park, CA:
Sage.

Dutton, D. G., & Golant, S. K. (1995). *The batterer: A psychological profile.* New
York: Basic Books.

Ehrmann, W. (1959). *Premarital dating behavior.* New York: Holt.

Emery, B. C. (1987). *Factors affecting attitudes towards premarital violence.* Un-
published doctoral dissertation, Oregon State University.

Emery, B. C., Cate, R. M., Henton, J. M., & Andrews, D. (1987, November). *Perceived legitimizing factors in premarital violence.* Paper presented at the Con-
ference of the National Council on Family Relations, Atlanta, GA.

Emery, B. C., & Lloyd, S. A. (1994). A feminist perspective on the study of
women who use aggression in close relationships. In D. L. Sollie & L. A.
Leslie (Eds.), *Gender, families and close relationships: Feminist research journeys* (pp. 237-262). Thousand Oaks, CA: Sage.

Estrich, S. (1987). *Real rape.* Cambridge, MA: Harvard University Press.

Felson, R. B., & Tedeschi, J. T. (1993). Social interactionist perspectives on ag-
gression and violence: An introduction. In R. B. Felson & J. T. Tedeschi
(Eds.), *Aggression and violence: Social interactionist perspectives* (pp. 1-10).
Washington, DC: American Psychological Association.

Ferraro, K. J. (1988). An existential approach to battering. In G. T. Hotaling,
D. Finkelhor, J. T. Kirkpatrick, & M. A. Straus (Eds.), *Family abuse and its*

consequences: New directions for research (pp. 126-138). Newbury Park, CA: Sage.

Ferraro, K. J., & Johnson, J. M. (1983). How women experience battering: The process of victimization. *Social Problems, 30,* 325-339.

Finley, C., & Corty, E. (1993). Rape on campus: The prevalence of sexual assault while enrolled in college. *Journal of College Student Development, 34,* 113-117.

Fisher, D. D. V. (1991). *An introduction to constructivism for social workers.* New York: Praeger.

Follingstad, D. R., Rutledge, L. L., Polek, D. S., & McNeil-Hawkins, K. (1988). Factors associated with patterns of dating violence toward college women. *Journal of Family Violence, 3,* 169-182.

Foo, L., & Margolin, G. (1995). A multivariate investigation of dating aggression. *Journal of Family Violence, 10,* 351-378.

Foshee, V., Bauman, K., & Linder, G. F. (1999). Family violence and the perpetration of adolescent dating violence: Examining social learning and social control processes. *Journal of Marriage and the Family, 61,* 331-342.

Foshee, V., & Linder, G. F. (1997). Factors influencing service provider motivation to help adolescent victims of partner violence. *Journal of Interpersonal Violence, 12,* 648-664.

Foucault, M. (1978). *The history of sexuality* (Vol. 1). New York: Pantheon.

Frazier, P. A., & Seales. L. M. (1997). Acquaintance rape is real rape. In M. D. Schwartz (Ed.), *Researching sexual violence against women: Methodological and personal perspectives* (pp. 54-55). Thousand Oaks, CA: Sage.

Gavey, N. (1992). Technologies and effects of heterosexual coercion. *Feminism and Psychology, 2,* 325-351.

Gavey, N. (1996). Women's desire and sexual violence discourse. In S. Wilkinson (Ed.), *Feminist social psychologies: International perspectives* (pp. 51-65). Philadelphia: Open University Press.

Gidycz, C. A., Hanson, K., & Layman, M. J. (1995). A prospective analysis of the relationship among sexual assault experiences: An extension of previous findings. *Psychology of Women Quarterly, 19,* 5-29.

Gilbert, N. (1993). Examining the facts: Advocacy research overstates the incidence of date and acquaintance rape. In R. J. Gelles & D. R. Loseke (Eds.), *Current controversies on family violence* (pp. 120-132). Newbury Park, CA: Sage.

Giles-Sims, J. (1983). *Wife battering: A systems theory approach.* New York: Guilford.

Glaser, B. G., & Strauss, A. L. (1967). *The discovery of grounded theory: Strategies for qualitative research.* New Brunswick, NJ: Transaction Books.

Glick, P., & Fiske, S. T. (1997). Hostile and benevolent sexism: Measuring ambivalent sexist attitudes toward women. *Psychology of Women Quarterly, 21,* 119-135.

Goldner, V., Penn, P., Sheinberg, M., & Walker, G. (1990). Love and violence: Gender paradoxes in volatile attachments. *Family Process, 29,* 343-364.

Goodman, L. A., Koss, M. P., Fitzgerald, L. F., Russo, N. F., & Keita, G. P. (1993). Male violence against women: Current research and future directions. *American Psychologist, 48,* 1054-1058.

Gordon, M. T., & Riger, S. (1989). *The female fear.* New York: Free Press.

Gortner, E. T., Gollan, J. K., & Jacobson, N. S. (1997). Psychological aspects of perpetrators of domestic violence and their relationships with their victims. *Psychiatric Clinics of North America, 20,* 337-352.

Gottman, J. M., Jacobson, N. S., Rushe, R. R., Shortt, J. W., Babcock, J., La Taillade, J. J., & Waltz, J. (1995). The relationship between heart rate reactivity, emotionally aggressive behavior, and general violence in batterers. *Journal of Family Psychology, 9,* 227-248.

Gray, H. M., & Foshee, V. (1997). Adolescent dating violence: Differences between one-sided and mutually violent profiles. *Journal of Interpersonal Violence, 12,* 126-141.

Griffin, S. (1981). *Pornography and silence.* New York: Harper & Row.

Gryl, F. E., Stith, S. M., & Bird, G. W. (1991). Close dating relationships among college students: Differences by use of violence and by gender. *Journal of Social and Personal Relationships, 8,* 243-264.

Gubrium, J. F., & Holstein, J. A. (1990). *What is family?* Mountain View, CA: Mayfield.

Gubrium, J. F., & Holstein, J. A. (1993a). Family discourse, organizational embeddedness and local enactment. *Journal of Family Issues, 14,* 66-81.

Gubrium, J. F., & Holstein, J. A. (1993b). Phenomenology, ethnomethodology, and family discourse. In P. G. Boss, W. J. Doherty, R. LaRossa, W. R. Schumm, & S. K. Steinmetz (Eds.), *Sourcebook of family theories and methods: A contextual approach* (pp. 651-675). New York: Plenum.

Gwartney-Gibbs, P. A., Stockard, J., & Boehmer, S. (1987). Learning courtship aggression: The influence of parents, peers, and personal experiences. *Family Relations, 36,* 276-282.

Hamby, S. L. (1996). The dominance scale: Preliminary psychometric properties. *Violence and Victims, 11,* 199-212.

Hammock, G., & Richardson, D. (1997). Perceptions of rape: The influence of closeness of relationship, intoxication and sex of participant. *Violence and Victims, 12,* 237-246.

Hanley, M. J., & O'Neill, P. (1997). Violence and commitment: A study of dating couples. *Journal of Interpersonal Violence, 12,* 685-703.

Harding, S. (1987). Is there a feminist method? In S. Harding (Ed.), *Feminism and methodology* (pp. 1-14). Bloomington: Indiana University Press.

Hare-Mustin, R. T. (1994). Discourses in the mirrored room: A postmodern analysis of therapy. *Family Process, 33,* 19-35.

Henley, N. M., Miller, M., & Beazley, J. A. (1995). Syntax, semantics and sexual violence: Agency and the passive voice. *Journal of Language and Social Psychology, 14,* 60-84.

Henton, J. M., Cate, R. M., Koval, J. E., Lloyd, S. A., & Christopher, F. S. (1983). Romance and violence in dating relationships. *Journal of Family Issues, 3,* 467-482.

Hersh, K., & Gray-Little, B. (1998). Psychopathic traits and attitudes associated with self-reported sexual aggression in college males. *Journal of Interpersonal Violence, 13,* 456-471.

Hickman, S. E., & Muehlenhard, C. L. (1997). College women's fears and precautionary behaviors relating to acquaintance rape and stranger rape. *Psychology of Women Quarterly, 21,* 527-547.

Hollway, W. (1989). *Subjectivity and method in psychology: Gender, meaning and science.* Newbury Park, CA: Sage.

Holstein, J. A., & Gubrium, J. F. (1995). Deprivatization and the construction of domestic life. *Journal of Marriage and the Family, 57,* 894-908.

Infante, D. A., Chandler, T. A., & Rudd, J. E. (1989). A test of an argumentative skill deficiency model of interspousal violence. *Communication Monographs, 56,* 163-177.

Jacobson, N. S., Gottman, J. M., Waltz, J., Rushe, R., Babcock, J., & Holtzworth-Munroe, A. (1994). Affect, verbal content, and psychophysiology in the arguments of couples with a violent husband. *Journal of Consulting and Clinical Psychology, 62,* 982-988.

Johnson, M. P. (1995). Patriarchal terrorism and common couple violence: Two forms of violence against women. *Journal of Marriage and the Family, 57,* 283-294.

Kahn, A. S., Mathie, V. A., & Torgler, C. (1994). Rape scripts and rape acknowledgment. *Psychology of Women Quarterly, 18,* 53-66.

Kalor, L. (1993). Dilemmas of femininity: Gender and the social construction of sexual imagery. *Sociological Quarterly, 34,* 639-651.

Kanin, E. J. (1957). Male aggression in dating-courting relations. *American Journal of Sociology, 63,* 197-204.

Kanin, E. J. (1985). Date rapists: Differential sexual socialization and relative deprivation. *Archives of Sexual Behavior, 14,* 219-231.

Kantor, G. K., & Straus, M. A. (1990). The "drunken bum" theory of wife beating. In M. A. Straus & R. J. Gelles (Eds.), *Physical violence in American families* (pp. 203-224). New Brunswick, NJ: Transaction Publishing.

Kaufman, G., Jr. (1992). The mysterious disappearance of battered women in family therapists' offices: Male privilege colluding with male violence. *Journal of Marital and Family Therapy, 18,* 233-243.

Kaufman, J., & Ziegler, E. (1987). Do abused children become abusive parents? *American Journal of Orthopsychiatry, 57,* 186-197.

Kelly, L. (1988a). How women define their experiences of violence. In K. Yllö & M. Bograd (Eds.), *Feminist perspectives on wife abuse* (pp. 114-132). Newbury Park, CA: Sage.

Kelly, L. (1988b). *Surviving sexual violence.* Minneapolis: University of Minnesota Press.

Kilpatrick, D. G., Best, C. L., Saunders, B. E., & Vernon, L. J. (1988). Rape in marriage and dating relationships: How bad is it for mental health? *Social Forces, 61,* 484-507.

Kirkwood, C. (1993). *Leaving abusive partners.* Newbury Park, CA: Sage.

Knudson-Martin, C., & Mahoney, A. R. (1996). Gender dilemmas and myth in the construction of marital bargains: Issues for marital therapy. *Family Process, 35,* 137-153.

Knudson-Martin, C., & Mahoney, A. R. (1998). Language and processes in the construction of equality in new marriages. *Family Relations, 47,* 81-91.

Korman, S. K., & Leslie, G. R. (1982). The relationship of feminist ideology and date expense sharing to perceptions of sexual aggression in dating. *Journal of Sex Research, 18,* 114-129.

Koss, M. P. (1988). Hidden rape: Sexual aggression and victimization in a national sample of students in higher education. In A. W. Burgess (Ed.), *Rape and sexual assault* (pp. 3-25). New York: Garland.

Koss, M. P. (1993a). Detecting the scope of rape: A review of prevalence research methods. *Journal of Interpersonal Violence, 8,* 198-222.

Koss, M. P. (1993b). Rape: Scope, impact, interventions and public policy responses. *American Psychologist, 48,* 1062-1069.

Koss, M. P., & Cleveland, H. H. (1997). Stepping on toes: Social roots of date rape lead to intractability and politizication. In M. D. Schwartz (Ed.), *Researching sexual violence against women: Methodological and personal perspectives* (pp. 4-20). Thousand Oaks, CA: Sage.

Koss, M. P., & Cook, S. L. (1993). Facing the facts: Date and acquaintance rape are significant problems for women. In R. J. Gelles & D. R. Loseke (Eds.), *Current controversies on family violence* (pp. 104-119). Newbury Park, CA: Sage.

Koss, M. P., & Dinero, T. E. (1989). Discriminant analysis of risk factors for sexual victimization among a sample of college women. *Family Relations, 57,* 242-250.

Koss, M. P., Dinero, T. E., Seibel, C. A., & Cox, S. L. (1988). Stranger and acquaintance rape: Are there differences in the victim's experiences? *Psychology of Women Quarterly, 12,* 1-24.

Koss, M. P., Gidycz, C. A., & Wisniewski, N. (1987). The scope of rape: Incidence and prevalence of sexual aggression and victimization in a national sample of higher education students. *Journal of Consulting and Clinical Psychology, 55,* 162-170.

Koss, M. P., Heise, L., & Russo, N. F. (1997). The global health burden of rape. In L. L. O'Toole & J. R. Schiffman (Eds.), *Gender violence: Interdisciplinary perspectives* (pp. 223-242). New York: New York University Press.

Koss, M. P., & Heslet, L. (1992). Somatic consequences of violence against women. *Archives of Family Medicine, 1,* 53-59.

Koss, M. P., & Oros, C. J. (1982). Sexual experiences survey: A research instrument investigating sexual aggression and victimization. *Journal of Consulting and Clinical Psychology, 50,* 455-457.

Kosson, D. S., Kelly, J. C., & White, J. W. (1997). Psychopathy-related traits predict self-reported sexual aggression among college men. *Journal of Interpersonal Violence, 12,* 241-254.

Kurz, D. (1997). Violence against women or family violence? Current debates. In L. L. O'Toole & J. R. Schiffman (Eds.), *Gender violence: Interdisciplinary perspectives* (pp. 443-453). New York: New York University Press.

Kurz, D. (1998). Old problems and new directions in the study of violence against women. In R. K. Bergen (Ed.), *Issues in intimate violence* (pp. 197-208). Thousand Oaks, CA: Sage.

Lamb, S. (1991). Acts without agents: An analysis of linguistic avoidance in journal articles on men who batter women. *American Journal of Orthopsychiatry, 61,* 250-257.

Lamb, S., & Keon, S. (1995). Blaming the perpetrator: Language that distorts reality in newspaper articles on men battering women. *Psychology of Women Quarterly, 19,* 209-220.

Laner, M. R. (1983). Courtship abuse and aggression: Contextual aspects. *Sociological Spectrum, 3,* 69-83.

Laner, M. R. (1990). Violence or its precipitators: Which is more likely to be identified a dating problem. *Deviant Behavior, 11,* 319-329.

Laner, M. R., & Thompson, J. (1982). Abuse and aggression in courting couples. *Deviant Behavior, 3,* 229-244.

Langley, J., Martin, J., & Nada-Raja, S. (1997). Physical assault among 21-year-olds by partners. *Journal of Interpersonal Violence, 12,* 675-684.

Lempert, L. B. (1996). Women's strategies for survival: Developing agency in abusive relationships. *Journal of Family Violence, 11,* 269-289.

Leonard, K. (1999). Alcohol use, alcohol abuse and marital aggression. In X. B. Arriaga & S. Oskamp (Eds.), *Violence in intimate relationships* (pp. 113-138). Thousand Oaks, CA: Sage.

Levant, R. F. (1995a). Male violence against female partners: Roots in male socialization and development. In C. D. Speilberger, I. G. Sarason, J. M. Brebner, E. Greenglass, P. Laungani, & A. M. O'Roark (Eds.), *Stress and emotion: Anxiety, anger and curiosity* (Vol. 15, pp. 91-100). Washington, DC: Taylor & Francis.

Levant, R. F. (1995b). Toward the reconstruction of masculinity. In R. F. Levant & W. S. Pollack (Eds.), *A new psychology of men* (pp. 229-251). New York: Basic Books.

Lloyd, S. A. (1991). The darkside of courtship. *Family Relations, 40,* 14-20.

Lloyd, S. A. (1996). Physical aggression and marital distress: The role of everyday marital interaction. In D. D. Cahn & S. A. Lloyd (Eds.), *Family violence from a communication perspective* (pp. 177-198). Thousand Oaks, CA: Sage.

Lloyd, S. A. (1999). The interpersonal and communication dynamics of wife battering. In X. Arriaga & S. Oskamp (Eds.), *Violence in intimate relationships* (99-111). Thousand Oaks, CA: Sage.

Lloyd, S. A., & Emery, B. C. (1993). Abuse in the family: An ecological, life cycle perspective. In T. H. Brubaker (Ed.), *Family relations: Challenges for the future* (pp. 129-152). Newbury Park, CA: Sage.

Lloyd, S. A., & Emery, B. C. (1994). Physically aggressive conflict in romantic relationships. In D. Cahn (Ed.), *Conflict in personal relationships* (pp. 27-46). Mahwah, NJ: Lawrence Erlbaum.

Lloyd, S. A., Koval, J. E. , & Cate, R. M. (1989). Conflict and violence in dating relationships. In M. Pirog-Good & J. Stets (Eds.), *Violence in dating relationships: Emerging social issues* (pp. 126-142). New York: Praeger.

Lundberg-Love, P., & Geffner, R. (1989). Date rape: Prevalence, risk factors, and a proposed model. In M. Pirog-Good & J. Stets (Eds.), *Violence in dating relationships: Emerging social issues* (pp. 169-184). New York: Praeger.

MacKinnon, C. (1982). Feminism, Marxism, method and the state: An agenda for theory. *Signs, 7*, 515-544.

Magdol, L., Moffitt, T. E., Caspi, A., & Silva, P. A. (1998). Hitting without a license: Testing explanations for difference in partner abuse between young adult daters and cohabitors. *Journal of Marriage and the Family, 60*, 41-55.

Mahoney, M. R. (1994). Victimization or oppression? Women's lives, violence and agency. In M. A. Fineman & R. Mykitiuk (Eds.), *The public nature of private violence* (pp. 59-92). Boston: Routledge & Kegan Paul.

Makepeace, J. M. (1981). Courtship violence among college students. *Family Relations, 30*, 97-102.

Makepeace, J. M. (1983). Life events stress and courtship violence. *Family Relations, 32*, 101-109.

Makepeace, J. M. (1986). Gender differences in courtship violence victimization. *Family Relations, 30*, 97-102.

Makepeace, J. M. (1987). Social factor and victim-offender differences in courtship violence. *Family Relations, 36*, 87-91.

Malamuth, N. M., & Brown, L. M. (1994). Sexually aggressive men's perceptions of women's communications: Testing three explanations. *Journal of Personality and Social Psychology, 67*, 699-712.

Malamuth, N. M., Sockloskie, R. J., Koss, M. P., & Tanaka, J. S. (1991). Characteristics of aggressors against women: Testing a model using a national sample of college students. *Journal of Consulting and Clinical Psychology, 59*, 670-681.

Malone, J., Tyree, A., & O'Leary, K. D. (1989). Generalization and containment: Different effects of past aggression for wives and husbands. *Journal of Marriage and the Family, 51*, 687-698.

Margolin, G., Burman, B. & John, R. S. (1989). Home observations of married couples reenacting naturalistic conflicts. *Behavioral Assessment, 11*, 101-118.

Margolin, G., John, R. S., & Gleberman, L. (1988). Affective responses to conflictual discussions in violent and nonviolent couples. *Journal of Consulting and Clinical Psychology, 56*, 24-33.

Marshall, L. L. (1994). Physical and psychological abuse. In W. R. Cupach & B. H. Spitzberg (Eds.), *The dark side of interpersonal communication* (pp. 281-311). Hillsdale, NJ: Lawrence Erlbaum.

Marshall, L. L., & Rose, P. (1987). Gender, stress and violence in the adult relationships of a sample of college students. *Journal of Social and Personal Relationships, 4*, 299-316.

Marshall, W. L., & Hambley, L. S. (1996). Intimacy and loneliness, and their relationship to rape myth acceptance and hostility toward women among rapists. *Journal of Interpersonal Violence, 11*, 586-592.

Martin, P. Y., & Hummer, R. A. (1998). Fraternities and rape on campus. In R. K. Bergen (Ed.), *Issues in intimate violence* (pp. 157-169). Thousand Oaks, CA: Sage.

Mason, A., & Blankenship, V. (1987). Power and affiliation motivation, stress and abuse in intimate relationships. *Journal of Personality and Social Psychology, 52*, 203-210.

Maynard, M. (1993). Violence towards women. In D. Richardson & V. Robinson (Eds.), *Thinking feminist: Key concepts in women's studies* (pp. 99-122). New York: Guilford.

Metts, S., & Spitzberg, B. (1996). Sexual communication in interpersonal contexts: A script-based approach. In B. R. Burleson (Ed.), *Communication yearbook 19* (pp. 49-91). Thousand Oaks, CA: Sage.

Meyers, M. (1997). *News coverage of violence against women.* Thousand Oaks, CA: Sage.

Morse, B. J. (1995). Beyond the Conflict Tactics Scale: Assessing gender differences in partner violence. *Violence and Victims, 10*, 251-272.

Motley, M. T., & Reeder, H. M. (1995). Unwanted escalation of sexual intimacy: Male and female perceptions of connotations and relational consequences of resistance messages. *Communication Monographs, 62*, 355-382.

Muehlenhard, C. L., Danoff-Burg, S., & Powch, I. G. (1996). Is rape sex or violence? Conceptual issues and implications. In D. M. Buss & N. M. Malamuth (Eds.), *Sex, power, conflict: Evolutionary and feminist perspectives* (pp. 119-137). New York: Oxford University Press.

Muehlenhard, C. L., & Hollabaugh, L. C. (1988). Do women sometimes say no when they mean yes: The prevalence and correlates of women's token resistance to sex. *Journal of Personality and Social Psychology 54*, 872-879.

Muehlenhard, C. L. & Linton, M. A. (1987). Date rape and sexual aggression in dating situations: Incidence and risk factors. *Journal of Counseling Psychology, 34*, 186-196.

NiCarthy, G. (1987). *The ones who got away.* Seattle: Seal.

Norris, J., & Cubbins, L. A. (1992). Dating, drinking and rape. *Psychology of Women Quarterly, 16,* 179-191.

Norris, J., Nurius, P. S., & Dimeff, L. A. (1996). Through her eyes: Factors affecting women's perception of and resistance to acquaintance and sexual aggression threat. *Psychology of Women Quarterly, 20,* 123-145.

Notz, M. P. (1984). Fantasy—testing—assessment: A proposed model for the investigation of mate selection. *Family Relations, 33,* 273-282.

O'Keefe, M. (1997). Predictors of dating violence among high school students. *Journal of Interpersonal Violence, 12,* 546-568.

O'Keefe, M. (1998). Factors mediating the link between witnessing interparental violence and dating violence. *Journal of Family Violence, 13,* 39-57.

O'Keefe, N. K., Brockopp, K., & Chew, E. (1986). Teen dating violence. *Social Work, 31,* 465-468.

O'Leary, K. D. (1988). Physical aggression between spouses: A social learning theory perspective. In V. B. Van Hasselt, R. L. Morrison, A. S. Bellack, & M. Hersen (Eds.), *Handbook of family violence* (pp. 11-55). New York: Plenum.

O'Leary, K. D., Barling, J., Arias, I., Rosenbaum, A., Malone, J., & Tyree, A. (1989). Prevalence and stability of physical aggression between spouses: A longitudinal analysis. *Journal of Consulting and Clinical Psychology, 57,* 263-268.

O'Leary, K. D., & Curley, A. D. (1986). Assertion and family violence: Correlates of spouse abuse. *Journal of Marital and Family Therapy, 12,* 281-290.

Osmond, M. W., & Thorne, B. (1993). Feminist theories: The social construction of gender in families and society. In P. G. Boss, W. J. Doherty, R. LaRossa, W. R. Schumm, & S. K. Steinmetz (Eds.), *Sourcebook of family theories and methods: A contextual approach* (pp. 591-625). New York: Plenum.

Paglia, C. (1995). Rape and the modern sex war. In A. M. Stan (Ed.), *Debating sexual correctness* (pp. 21-25). New York: Delta.

Pare, D. A. (1996). Culture and meaning: Expanding the metaphorical repertoire of family therapy. *Family Process, 35,* 21-42.

Peplau, L. A. (1994). Men and women in love. In D. L. Sollie & L. A. Leslie (Eds.), *Gender, families and close relationships: Feminist research journeys* (pp. 19-49). Thousand Oaks, CA: Sage.

Peplau, L. A., Rubin, Z., & Hill, C. T. (1977). Sexual intimacy in dating relationships. *Journal of Social Issues, 33,* 86-109.

Pleck, E. H. (1987). *Domestic tyranny: The making of social policy against family violence from colonial times to the present.* New York: Oxford University Press.

Pollitt, K. (1995). Not just bad sex. In A. M. Stan (Ed.), *Debating sexual correctness* (pp. 162-171). New York: Delta.

Ptacek, J. (1988). Why do men batter their wives? In K. Yllö & M. Bograd (Eds.), *Feminist perspectives on wife abuse* (pp. 133-157). Newbury Park, CA: Sage.

Reiss, D. (1981). *The family's construction of reality.* Cambridge, MA: Harvard University Press.

Resick, P. A. (1993). The psychological impact of rape. *Journal of Interpersonal Violence, 8,* 223-255.

Riggs, D. S. (1993). Relationship problems and dating aggression: A potential treatment target. *Journal of Interpersonal Violence, 8,* 18-35.

Riggs, D. S., & Caulfield, M. B. (1997). Expected consequences of male violence against their female dating partners. *Journal of Interpersonal Violence, 12,* 229-240.

Riggs, D. S., & O'Leary, K. D. (1996). Aggression between heterosexual dating partners. *Journal of Interpersonal Violence, 11,* 519-540.

Rogers, L. E., Castleton, A., & Lloyd, S. A. (1996). Relational control and physical aggression in satisfying marital relationships. In D. D. Cahn & S. A. Lloyd (Eds.), *Family violence from a communication perspective* (pp. 218-239). Thousand Oaks, CA: Sage.

Roiphe, K. (1995). Date rape's other victim. In A. M. Stan (Ed.), *Debating sexual correctness* (pp. 149-161). New York: Delta.

Ronfeldt, H. M., Kimerling, R., & Arias, I. (1998). Satisfaction with relationship power and the perpetration of dating violence. *Journal of Marriage and the Family, 60,* 70-78.

Roscoe, B., & Benaske, N. (1985). Courtship violence experienced by abused wives: Similarities in patterns of abuse. *Family Relations, 34,* 419-424.

Rosen, K. H. (1996). The ties that bind women to violent premarital relationships: Processes of seduction and entrapment. In D. D. Cahn & S. A. Lloyd (Eds.), *Family violence from a communication perspective* (pp. 151-176). Thousand Oaks, CA: Sage.

Rosen, K. H., & Bird, K. (1996). A case of woman abuse: Gender ideologies, power paradoxes and unresolved conflict. *Violence Against Women, 2,* 302-321.

Rosen, K. H., & Stith, S. (1993). Intervention strategies for treating women in violent dating relationships. *Family Relations, 42,* 427-433.

Rubin, Z., Peplau, L. A., & Hill, C. T. (1981). Loving and leaving: Sex differences in romantic attachments. *Sex Roles, 7,* 821-835.

Russell, D. (1984). *Sexual exploitation.* Beverly Hills, CA: Sage.

Sabourin, T. C. (1995). The role of negative reciprocity in spouse abuse: A relational control analysis. *Journal of Applied Communication, 23,* 271-283.

Saunders, D. G. (1988). Wife abuse, husband abuse, or mutual combat. In K. Yllö & M. Bograd (Eds.), *Feminist perspectives on wife abuse* (pp. 90-113). Newbury Park, CA: Sage.

Sawicki, J. (1991). *Disciplining Foucault: Feminism, power, and the body.* Boston: Routledge & Kegan Paul.

Schaeffer, A. M., & Nelson, W. S. (1993). Rape-supportive attitudes: Effects of on-campus residence and education. *Journal of College Student Development, 34,* 175-179.

Schwartz, M. D. (1987). Gender and injury in spousal assault. *Sociological Focus, 20,* 61-75.

Schwartz, M. D., & DeKeseredy, W. S. (1997). *Sexual assault on the college campus: The role of male peer support.* Thousand Oaks, CA: Sage.

Serra, P. (1993). Physical violence in the couple relationship: A contribution toward the analysis of context. *Family Process, 32,* 21-33.

Shapiro, B. L., & Schwarz, J. C. (1997). Date rape: Its relationship to trauma symptoms and sexual self-esteem. *Journal of Interpersonal Violence, 12,* 407-419.

Shotland, R. L. (1989). A model of the causes of date rape in developing and close relationships. In C. Hendrick (Ed.), *Close relationships* (pp. 247-270). Newbury Park, CA: Sage.

Shotland, R. L. (1992). A theory of the causes of courtship rape: Part 2. *Journal of Social Issues, 48,* 127-143.

Simons, R. L., Lin, K., & Gordon, L. C. (1998). Socialization in the family of origin and male dating violence: A prospective study. *Journal of Marriage and the Family, 60,* 467-478.

Small, S. A., & Kerns, D. (1993). Unwanted sexual activity among peers during early and middle adolescence: Incidence and risk factors. *Journal of Marriage and the Family, 55,* 941-952.

Smith, J. P., & Williams, J. G. (1992). From abusive household to dating violence. *Journal of Family Violence, 7,* 153-165.

Spitzberg, B. H. (1997). Violence in intimate relationships. In W. R. Cupach & D. J. Canary (Eds.), *Competence in interpersonal conflict* (pp. 175-201). New York: McGraw-Hill.

Spitzberg, B. H. (1998). Sexual coercion in courtship relations. In B. H. Spitzberg & W. R. Cupach (Eds.), *The dark side of close relationships* (pp. 179-232). Mahwah, NJ: Lawrence Erlbaum.

Sprecher, S., & Felmlee, D. (1997). The balance of power in romantic relationships: Heterosexual couples over time from "his" and "her" perspectives. *Sex Roles, 37,* 361-379.

Stamp, G. H., & Sabourin, T. C. (1995). Accounting for violence: An analysis of male spousal abuse narratives. *Journal of Applied Communication Research, 23,* 284-307.

Stanko, E. A. (1997). "I second that emotion": Reflections on feminism, emotionality, and research on sexual violence. In M. D. Schwartz (Ed.), *Researching sexual violence against women: Methodological and personal perspectives* (pp. 74-84). Thousand Oaks, CA: Sage.

Stermac, L., DuMont, J., & Dunn, S. (1998). Violence in known-assailant sexual assaults. *Journal of Interpersonal Violence, 13,* 398-412.

Stets, J. E. (1988). *Domestic violence and control.* New York: Springer-Verlag.

Stets, J. E. (1991). Cohabiting and marital aggression: The role of social isolation. *Journal of Marriage and the Family, 53,* 669-680.

Stets, J. E. (1992). Interactive processes in dating aggression: A national study. *Journal of Marriage and the Family, 54*, 165-177.

Stets, J. E., & Henderson, D. A. (1991). Contextual factors surrounding conflict resolution while dating: Results from a national study. *Family Relations, 40*, 29-36.

Stets, J. E., & Pirog-Good, M. A. (1989). Sexual aggression and control in dating relationships. *Journal of Applied Social Psychology, 19*, 1392-1412.

Stets, J. E., & Pirog-Good, M. A. (1990). Interpersonal control and courtship aggression. *Journal of Social and Personal Relationships, 7*, 371-394.

Stets, J. E., & Straus, M. A. (1990). Gender differences in reporting marital violence and its medical and social consequences. In M. A. Straus & R. J. Gelles (Eds.), *Physical violence in American families* (pp. 151-166). New Brunswick, NJ: Transaction.

Steward, S. (1995). Absolute seduction. In C. Carter (Ed.), *The other side of silence: Women tell about their experiences with date rape* (pp. 51-60). Gilsum, NH: Avocus.

Stock, W. (1991). Feminist explanations: Male power, hostility, and sexual coercion. In E. Grauerholz & M. A. Koralewski (Eds.), *Sexual coercion: A sourcebook on its nature, causes, and prevention* (pp. 61-73). Lexington, MA: Lexington Books.

Straus, M. A. (1979). Measuring intrafamily conflict and violence: The Conflict Tactics (CT) Scale. *Journal of Marriage and the Family, 41*, 75-90.

Straus, M. A., & Gelles, R. J. (1990). How violent are American families? Estimates from the national family violence resurvey and other studies. In M. A. Straus & R. J. Gelles (Eds.), *Physical violence in American families* (pp. 95-112). New Brunswick, NJ: Transaction.

Straus, M. A., Gelles, R. J., & Steinmetz, S. (1979). *Behind closed doors: Violence in the American family*. New York: Basic Books.

Strauss, A. L., & Corbin, J. (1990). *Basics of qualitative research*. Newbury Park, CA: Sage.

Sugarman, D. B., & Hotaling, G. T. (1989). Dating violence: Prevalence, context, and risk markers. In M. A. Pirog-Good & J. E. Stets (Eds.), *Violence in dating relationships: Emerging social issues* (pp. 3-32). New York: Praeger.

Tannen, D. (1990). *You just don't understand: Women and men in conversation*. New York: Ballantine.

Thompson, L. (1992). Feminist methodology for family studies. *Journal of Marriage and the Family, 54*, 3-18.

Thompson, L., & Walker, A. J. (1995). The place of feminism in family studies. *Journal of Marriage and the Family, 57*, 847-865.

Tyler, K., Hoyt, D., & Whitbeck, L. (1998). Coercive sexual strategies. *Violence and Victims, 13*, 47-61.

Umberson, D., Anderson, K., Glick, J., & Shapiro, A. (1998). Domestic violence, personal control, and gender. *Journal of Marriage and the Family, 60*, 442-452.

Walker, L. E. (1979). *The battered woman*. New York: Harper & Row.

Waller, W. (1937). The rating and dating complex. *American Sociological Review, 2,* 727-734.

Waller, W. (1951). *The family: A dynamic interpretation*. New York: Dryden.

Warshaw, R. (1988). *I never called it rape*. New York: Harper & Row.

Weedon, C. (1987). *Feminist practice and poststructuralist theory*. Oxford, UK: Basil Blackwell.

Weingarten, K. (1991). The discourses of intimacy: Adding a social constructionist and feminist view. *Family Process, 30,* 285-305.

West, C., & Zimmerman, D. H. (1991). Doing gender. In J. Lorber & S. A. Farrell (Eds.), *The social construction of gender* (pp. 13-37). Newbury Park, CA: Sage.

Wetherell, M. (1995). Romantic discourse and feminist analysis: Interrogating investment, power, and desire. In S. Wilkinson & C. Kitzinger (Eds.), *Feminism and discourse: Psychological perspectives* (pp. 128-144). Thousand Oaks, CA: Sage.

Whitchurch, G. G., & Constantine, L. L. (1993). Systems theory. In P. G. Boss, W. J. Doherty, R. LaRossa, W. R. Schumm, & S. K. Steinmetz (Eds.), *Sourcebook of family theories and methods: A contextual approach* (pp. 325-352). New York: Plenum.

Widom, C. (1989). Does violence beget violence? A critical examination of the literature. *Psychological Bulletin, 106,* 3-28.

Wiehe, V. R., & Richards, A. L. (1995). *Intimate betrayal: Understanding and responding to the trauma of acquaintance rape*. Thousand Oaks, CA: Sage.

Willbach, D. (1989). Ethics and family therapy: The case management of family violence. *Journal of Marriage and Family Therapy, 15,* 43-52.

Worth, D. M., Matthews, P. A., & Coleman, W. R. (1990). Sex role, group affiliation, family background, and courtship violence in college students. *Journal of College Student Development, 31,* 250-254.

Yllö, K. (1988). Political and methodological debates in wife abuse research. In K. Yllö & M. Bograd (Eds.), *Feminist perspectives on wife abuse* (pp. 28-50). Newbury Park, CA: Sage.

Yllö, K. (1994). Reflections of a feminist family violence researcher. In D. A. Sollie & L. A. Leslie (Eds.), *Gender, families, and close relationships: Feminist research journeys* (pp. 213-236). Thousand Oaks, CA: Sage.

Zweig, J. M., Barber, B. L., & Eccles, J. S. (1997). Sexual coercion and well-being in young adulthood. *Journal of Interpersonal Violence, 12,* 291-308.

Author Index

Subject Index

About the Authors

Sally A. Lloyd is Director of Women's Studies and Professor of Educational Leadership at Miami University in Oxford, Ohio. She earned her Ph.D. at Oregon State University in 1982. Her teaching and scholarship center on violence against women, the interpersonal dynamics of violent relationships, feminism, and conflict and control in both courtship and marriage. She is the coeditor (with D. D. Cahn) of *Family Violence From a Communication Perspective,* which received the Distinguished Book Award from the Applied Communication Division of the Speech Communication Association.

Beth C. Emery is Professor of Child Development and Family Studies in the Human Sciences Department at Middle Tennessee State University in Murfreesboro. She earned her Ph.D. from Oregon State University in 1987. Her teaching and scholarship focus on violence against women, interpersonal communication, feminism, and families at risk.